AF872654

Bleeding in the Pews

The Church's Kairos Moment

Michael J Menard

UACT Press

Copyright © 2026 by Michael J Menard

All rights reserved.

ISBNs
Paperback: 978-1-968559-12-0
Hardcover: 978-1-968559-13-7
ebook: 978-1-968559-14-4

No portion of this book may be reproduced in any form without written permission from the publisher or author, except as permitted by U.S. copyright law.

Published by UACT Press

Praise for

Bleeding in the Pews

Faith Heals

For more than 40 years, my research at Duke University has focused on a single question: What is the relationship between religious faith and human health? Across nearly 700 peer-reviewed studies and 70 books, the evidence has been overwhelming—religious involvement is consistently associated with better outcomes in depression, substance abuse, suicide prevention, and recovery from trauma. The science is clear. Faith heals.

However, the very institutions best positioned to deliver that healing often cannot see the wounds sitting right in front of them.

That is the crisis Michael Menard exposes in *Bleeding in the Pews*, and he does it with a rare combination of scientific rigor, pastoral compassion, and personal courage that I have seldom encountered. Menard's central argument—that childhood trauma is a neurobiological wound the church has been misdiagnosing as a spiritual failure—is not only correct, but also decades overdue.

This book deserves the widest possible audience.

–Harold G. Koenig, M.D., M.H.Sc.

Professor of Psychiatry and Behavioral Sciences, Duke University Medical Center; Director, Center for Spirituality, Theology and Health

God Heals and Uses Helpers

Michael Menard has an extraordinary ability to synthesize faith, trauma psychology, and neuroscience—and show how hidden wounds from childhood trauma can more deeply heal when all three are accessed. Drawing upon his remarkable service in the corporate world, he describes a path forward for everyday people and leaders to make their faith communities even more effective sanctuaries of healing, joy, and peace. As Menard wisely explains: Heal the brain wiring damaged by trauma and divine grace and love can flow unimpeded. This is a must-read for all people of faith who care about their own wellbeing, their marriages, and the wellbeing of their neighbors in the pews and beyond.

–Glenn R. Schiraldi, Ph.D., Lt. Col. (USA, Ret.)
University of Maryland School of Public Health (retired; presently adjunct); author of fourteen books, including The Adverse Childhood Experiences Recovery Workbook and The Post-Traumatic Stress Disorder Sourcebook

We Cannot Train Enough Therapists

The mental health crisis facing our communities is so widespread it is increasingly understood as a matter of public health. Trauma is not something "out there" for churches to address—trauma is already within the walls of our churches. Many of us just don't know it yet. *Bleeding in the Pews* is a compelling, thorough, and practical resource. I wholeheartedly recommend this book.

–David C. Wang, Th.M., Ph.D.
Cliff and Joyce Penner Chair for the Formation of Emotionally Healthy Leaders; Professor of Psychology and Spiritual Formation, Fuller Theological Seminary

Healed People Help Heal People

As a little girl growing up in Africa, it felt like my people were bleeding from pain, addiction, trauma, and poverty. Yet the message from the church was, "Come sit in our pews, sing our songs—but just keep bleeding." *Bleeding in the Pews* is a hopeful and timely invitation to the Church. This book is a love letter to the Church and an invitation to experience the healing Christ died to give us.

–Kate Drayton

Founder, Flourishing Lifeway; SAMHSA-certified trauma-informed trainer

Stethoscopes and Scalpels

Bleeding in the Pews delivers the diagnosis the church desperately needs—naming the hidden epidemic of trauma that haunts our pews. Michael Menard writes not as a theologian, but as a relentless researcher who places trauma-responsive stethoscopes and scalpels in the hands of preachers, teachers, and lay leaders, and makes the case that the local church was designed to be a spiritual hospital for the suffering. A critical catalyst for revival in the 21st century.

–Robert L. Briggs

Co-founder, Alliance Practice; former President and CEO, American Bible Society

A Roadmap for Faith Leaders

With both urgency and compassion, Michael Menard challenges churches to recognize the widespread impact of trauma and to become places of understanding, connection, and healing. This book is both an urgent wake-up call and a roadmap for faith leaders seeking to build healthier congregations and stronger communities.

–Meri McCoy-Thompson

Executive Director, Dovetail Learning; co-author of The Heart of Resilience

An Unambiguous Trumpet Call

Michael Menard sounds an unambiguous trumpet call. He takes complex neuroscience and makes it impossible to miss—even a reader with no scientific background will grasp it fully. He doesn't dumb it down; he culturally adapts it with illustrations and examples that are genuinely brilliant. What impressed me most is that Menard consistently affirms the centrality and purpose of the church as it was always intended to be, while closing every legitimate theological escape hatch. And then he goes further—he offers a clear, actionable pathway for becoming a trauma-responsive church. After reading this book, ignorance is no longer an excuse.

–Jeff Adams, Ph.D.

International ministry leader, educator, and leadership consultant across eighty countries on six continents

Imagine Trauma-Responsive Clergy

Imagine a world where the clergy are trauma responsive. Such a book could change and save lives. Well-written and researched. I am glad this book exists, and I am buying copies for my local clergymen.

–Monica Smith

Addiction recovery program facilitator and C-PTSD thriver

Other Books by

Michael J Menard

A Fish in Your Ear

Corporate Transformation

The Kite That Couldn't Fly

Greater Than Gravity

Whispers of Hope

Contents

KAIROS

(καιρός) • noun • \ˈkī-ˌräs\

Ancient Greek: "The appointed time"

The supreme moment when conditions align for decisive action that cannot be delayed or repeated.

Unlike Chronos, which measures the relentless march of time, Kairos marks the pregnant instant when time itself holds its breath—when divine opportunity intersects human readiness, when the window opens that will not stay open, when what has always been possible suddenly becomes urgent and unavoidable.

In Greek mythology, Kairos was depicted as a young man with wings on his feet and a single lock of hair falling over his forehead. To grasp that forelock is to seize destiny. To let him pass is to watch opportunity vanish forever—for the back of his head is bald. There is nothing to grab once he has gone by.

The early church understood Kairos as the moment when Christ entered history—not merely another day on the calendar, but the day when everything changed. The fullness of time. God's appointed hour.

This is the church's Kairos moment.

The opposite of Kairos is not merely delay—it is deafness to the appointed hour, blindness to the open door, the fatal confusion of someday with now.

> "To everything there is a season, and a time to every purpose under heaven."
>
> –Ecclesiastes 3:1

Foreword

When Bobbie Wright first became part of our church family, I was warned to keep my eyes on her.

She had been part of the congregation that met in the building we acquired, and according to the last pastor, was single-handedly responsible for most of the drama that ultimately led to his resignation. She was eighty years old, running her late husband's heavy equipment company with an iron fist. In one of my first conversations with her, she told me she was glad her husband was dead, and that she "hoped he is burning in hell."

Nice to meet you, too, Miss Bobbie.

A year later, Miss Bobbie told me something she had never told another living person. When she was fifteen years old, she was already married and pregnant. Her husband dropped her off at an illegal abortion clinic in an alley in Detroit. He picked her up a couple of hours later, but she left behind the baby that had been living inside her womb. They didn't speak of it then. They never spoke of it again.

She had been living with the trauma of that experience for sixty-five years. It hadn't gone away. It had simply been stuffed somewhere deep inside her, buried beneath the weight of shame for something she never had any real control over. She was fifteen. It was the 1950s. She felt she had no choice but to obey her husband.

Childhood trauma is a wound and wounds bleed. Miss Bobbie was bleeding in the pews.

She is one of countless people I have encountered as a pastor who were wounded deeply and handed a bandage to cover it up.

I knew something of this myself.

When I was eight years old, I cut my knee open with a machete doing yard work while my father slept. He had been addicted to prescription pain medicine long before the world had a name for that. I was bleeding profusely. The cut was so deep I could see bone from my knee joint and the nerve endings that had been severed, bouncing around in the wound. I woke my father, knowing he was going to be angry, but I was more afraid of bleeding to death than being yelled at.

My father carried his own childhood trauma—the inheritance of an alcoholic, physically abusive father. By the time he was eighteen, he had lied about having epilepsy on an Army enlistment application just to get out of the house. In his mind, Vietnam was safer than home. Groggy-eyed and with an unsteady hand, my father used every bandage in the house to try to press the edges of the wound together. Then he went back to sleep. It was eleven in the morning.

By noon, the blood had soaked through the makeshift dressing and was seeping into my socks and onto the floor. I would eventually need fifteen stitches. We never spoke of it again.

All the bandages in the world couldn't heal that wound. What I needed was not a covering, but a cure. The wound had to be treated, not concealed.

That physical wound became a metaphor for the emotional wounds I carried growing up in the home of an addict. For years I covered them the only way I knew how—with relentless ambition and the pursuit of success. I became deeply involved in the music industry and eventually landed at William Morris Agency, one of the largest talent agencies in the world. By any external measure, I was winning.

But I was still bleeding. Into my marriage. Into my parenting. Into the people around me. The bandages of hard work and achievement couldn't stop it.

Like Miss Bobbie, Shannon and I were faithful church members. We sat in the pews. We tithed. We volunteered every time a need arose. We showed up and we gave everything we had.

And yet my wife was lonelier than ever. My kids knew what I *thought* about everything under the sun, but didn't know how I *felt*. I was present in the building yet absent in the home. The bandages—showing up and serving—couldn't stop the bleeding.

That is the story of countless people sitting in pews all over the world. Faithful. Committed. And still hemorrhaging inside, where no one can see it.

In 2010, God called me to sell my company and plant a church in Middle Tennessee. I was now the pastor. I was preaching every Sunday. I was traveling the world fighting on behalf of the poor and powerless—sometimes literally. It was meaningful, vital work.

And it was another bandage.

Shannon was in the front row while I was behind the pulpit. And neither of us fully understood she was carrying wounds from her own childhood that decades of faith, service, and devotion had never reached. I was up on that platform proclaiming the grace of God every week while my own wife was bleeding invisibly in the front row.

That is not a comfortable thing to write, but it is the truth. And the truth is exactly what this book demands.

The church had given us both the same prescription it gives everyone: pray more, believe more, serve more. We followed it faithfully. And it was not enough. Not because the Gospel is insufficient, but because we were treating a neurobiological wound with spiritual aspirin, and calling it healing.

Shannon's journey—the courage it has taken her to name what happened to her, to seek the healing the church alone could not provide, and to allow her story to be told in these pages—is one of the most remarkable things I have ever witnessed. She has shown me what it looks like to truly stop bleeding. Not by trying harder or believing more, but by finally treating the actual wound.

I owe her more than I can put into words.

I had been around ministry long enough to watch pastors, some of my closest friends among them, fall into moral failures that destroyed their marriages, their families, and their churches. I was not smarter or more gifted than any of them. That realization scared me enough to look honestly at my own soul. It was then that I began the real work: identifying the wounds I had been covering and allowing God to actually heal them rather than continuing to manage them.

The change has been unmistakable. I still go to some of the most dangerous places on earth to fight on behalf of the most vulnerable. I still lead the church God called me to plant. But I no longer do it out of a deep, subconscious compulsion to fill a hole left by my father. I do it now from the overflow of a life that is genuinely being healed. My ministry is no longer manic and chaotic. It is steady. And it is more effective than it has ever been.

When Michael Menard first told me about the work he had been doing, I had to be part of it. We are at a remarkable moment. Much of the stigma surrounding emotional suffering caused by childhood trauma has begun to lift. Awareness is rising. The conversation is reaching places it never reached before, including the pews of churches like mine. That is good, but awareness is only the beginning. The question that haunts me as a pastor is not "Do we know that people are hurting?" We have always known that. The real question is "What do we actually do about it?"

In Africa, I have helped drill clean water wells, because dirty water is what is killing people. You can hand out medicine, run campaigns, and raise awareness about waterborne disease until the end of time, but until you address the source of the contamination, people keep dying.

Childhood trauma is the clean water issue of our country. As Michael documents in these pages, it is not a peripheral social problem. It is the root system beneath our addiction crisis, our suicide epidemic, our mental health emergency, and so much more. It is killing our children. It is killing our parents. It is sitting, invisible and untreated, in the pews of every church in America.

It is time to stop handing out bandages. It is time to drill wells of healing in the hearts and souls of our people.

That time is now.

As you read the pages that follow, I want to invite you to be honest. Honest about the wounds you are still carrying. Honest about the people sitting around you who are carrying their own. Honest about what the church has offered and what it has not.

Michael Menard is not writing this book to condemn the church. He loves the church. I love the church. But love requires us to see clearly. And what we have not been seeing clearly is the bleeding in the pews.

My prayer is that you will find healing in these pages. And that as you do, you will join the fight to make sure no one around you has to keep bleeding alone.

Darren Tyler
Founding Pastor, Conduit Church
Franklin, Tennessee

“For I desire mercy, not sacrifice.”

–Hosea 6:6

Introduction

The Gods Are Angry

Zara saw it first. She was maybe 14, standing outside the cave entrance at dusk, watching the sky darken while the others settled inside—her mother scraping hides, her father sharpening stone, the younger ones already asleep on piles of grass and fur. But Zara stayed outside because she'd been watching the white circle in the sky for months now, and she'd figured something out: it changed.

Every night, a little different. Sometimes fat and full, lighting up the whole valley so she could see the shadows of trees and the shapes of animals moving in the distance. Other times, just a sliver—barely enough light to see her own hand. And here's what she noticed: her body changed with it. When the circle was full, her belly cramped and she bled. Every single time. Twenty-nine days, and the cycle repeated.

She told her mother, and her mother just nodded like she'd known all along. "We all do," she said. "We follow the sky."

Zara didn't know what that meant, but she felt it. Something up there—something big and powerful and beyond her control—was connected to what happened down here. To her body. To the rhythm of her life.

And if it controlled her blood, what else did it control?

That same night, across the valley, a man named Kael stood at the edge of the forest with three other hunters, waiting for the full moon. They'd learned that when the white circle was whole, the antelope grazed longer in the open. The light made them careless, and that meant meat. But when the sky was dark, the animals stayed hidden. The hunts failed. Bellies stayed empty. Children cried through the night.

Kael didn't understand why the light came and went. He just knew it mattered. The sky decided whether they ate or starved. And slowly, over seasons and generations, a belief took root: whatever controls the light controls everything.

Then came the rain. When it fell, green shoots pushed up through the dirt—plants the people learned to gather and eat, roots they could dig up and store. When the rain came, there was food. When it didn't, the plants shriveled, the streams dried up, and the people grew weak.

One summer, the rain stopped for 90 days. The elder, a woman named Ita, stood in the center of the group and said what everyone was thinking: "We've done something wrong."

No one argued. It made sense. The sky gave rain when it wanted to. And now it had stopped. So they must have angered it.

Ita led them to a flat rock near the river—a place they'd come to think of as sacred. She told the others to bring their best: the ripest berries, the fattest roots, a piece of meat from the last successful hunt. They laid it all on the rock and waited.

Three days later, it rained. Not much—just enough to dampen the ground and coax a few plants back to life. But it was enough to confirm what Ita suspected: the offering worked. The sky forgave them.

From that day forward, they gave thanks every time things went well. And when things went wrong—when the rain didn't come or sickness swept through the group—they didn't wonder if maybe it was just chance. They assumed they hadn't given enough. So they gave more. More food. More time. More energy spent on rituals they hoped would make the sky happy again.

And when that didn't work, they gave blood.

Kael's son, a boy of maybe 16, was the first. The drought had lasted six months. So the boy stood on the sacred rock, took a sharpened stone, and cut his own arm, letting the blood drip onto the stone while the others watched in silence. Two days later, it rained.

And then, one terrible season when the rain didn't come for a full year and half the children died, someone suggested the unthinkable: "What if we gave a child?"

The logic was brutal but clear. If the gods controlled everything, and if they were this angry, then maybe food and blood weren't enough. Maybe they wanted a life.

So a mother—no one remembers her name, but the story says she volunteered—wrapped her newborn in soft hides, laid the baby on the sacred rock, and let the men light the fire.

The baby didn't make a sound. The rain came three days later.

What began as a desperate act in one starving tribe became ritual in another, then doctrine in the next. Over centuries and millennia, some civilizations made human sacrifice a constant obligation. The Aztecs built an empire on it—capturing warriors from rival tribes, marching them up temple steps by the thousands, cutting out their still-beating hearts to feed the sun god so he would have the strength to rise each morning.

We call this primitive. We teach it in schools as ancient superstition—evidence of how far we've come. But here's what we don't talk about: those beliefs didn't just disappear. They didn't evaporate when we built cities or wrote laws or discovered that rain comes from condensation, not divine mood swings. Those beliefs—do more, give more, sacrifice more, or the gods will punish you—were encoded into the structure of our brains since the beginning of time. They became the foundation of every religion that followed, including ours.

We don't sacrifice children on rocks anymore. But walk into a church on any given Sunday, and you'll hear the same ancient logic, dressed up in different words: pray harder, believe better, give more, serve faithfully, submit completely. And if you're still suffering—if you're still anxious, still depressed, still haunted by something you can't name—well, maybe you're not doing enough. Maybe God is still angry. Maybe you need to sacrifice more.

We say Jesus came to end the cycle of sacrifice. "It is finished," He said on the cross. No more offerings. No more blood. No more trying to earn what's already been given.

But try telling that to the woman in the third row who's been praying for 20 years for her depression to lift. Try telling that to the man in the back who serves on three committees, leads a small group, tithes faithfully, and still wakes up every morning wanting to die. Try telling that to the teenager sitting in youth group, smiling on the outside, bleeding on the inside, convinced that if she just had more faith, God would fix whatever's broken in her.

The gods are still angry. At least, that's what we've been taught to believe. So we keep sacrificing—our time, our energy, our mental health, our hope—trying to appease a God who was never the problem in the first place.

My Story

I know this because I lived it. I grew up one of 14 children in Kankakee, Illinois, in a home where chaos was the weather and survival was the only skill that mattered. I carried childhood trauma for decades without knowing what it was—just a persistent brokenness I couldn't pray away, outwork, or silence no matter how much I achieved.

I came to this work not as a pastor or clinician, but as someone trained to diagnose why complex systems fail and what it takes to fix them. Four decades in global corporate leadership taught me one thing above all: Institutions resist what they most need. That diagnostic lens turns out to be exactly what this conversation requires.

I lost two brothers to heroin addiction—Adam and Patrick—both dead from wounds that started in childhood. I watched the strongest people I knew be destroyed by something no one could name and no church knew how to treat.

When I finally discovered the science of childhood trauma—the ACE Study, the neuroscience, the research that explained everything I'd lived through—it hit me like a freight train. Not just for myself, but for the 180 million Americans carrying the same invisible wounds. Sitting in the same pews. Hearing the same prescription: try harder, believe more, sacrifice more.

The gods were never angry. And the problem was never faith. The problem is a wound that no amount of sacrifice will heal.

The Crisis No One Sees

Childhood trauma is an epidemic hiding in plain sight. It impacts 180 million adults and 50 million children in America alone. It is the number one contributor to addiction, suicide, and incarceration. It is sitting in the pews of every church in this country, invisible and untreated, while we keep handing out the same ancient prescription.

The church can't see it. Not because it doesn't care, but because no one taught it to look. Pastors see the symptoms—the anger, the anxiety, the addiction, the inability to trust or connect or rest—but they don't see the source. They treat it as a spiritual problem requiring spiritual solutions, when what's actually broken is neurobiological. A brain rewired by childhood terror. A nervous system stuck in permanent survival mode. A body that remembers what the mind has tried to forget.

The church isn't the villain of this story. The church is blind. And there's a difference. Cruelty sees the wound and inflicts more pain. Blindness can't see the wound at all, so it prescribes remedies that don't work and sometimes make things worse.

What God Thinks of This

I need to say something the rest of this book does not say plainly enough:

This is evil.

Not the church's failure to see it—that is blindness, and blindness can be healed. I mean the wounding itself. The hand raised against a child. The voice that tells a six-year-old she is worthless. The parent who disappears. The adult who uses a child for their own appetite. The household where a child learns the people who are supposed to be safe are the ones to fear.

There is no neutral way to describe what is being done to a child when their developing brain is rewired by terror. It is not a misfortune. It is not a statistic. It is a small bomb planted in a child's mind that will detonate for decades, often for the rest of their life, and Scripture does not mince words about how God feels about the people who plant it.

Jesus said this: *"If anyone causes one of these little ones who believe in me to stumble, it would be better for them to have a large millstone hung around their neck and to be drowned in the depths of the sea."* (Matthew 18:6)

Read that again. Drowning is the gentler outcome.

A millstone in the first century weighed hundreds of pounds. The image is not poetic. It is graphic on purpose. There is a hierarchy of things that grieve God, and at the very top of that hierarchy sits the harm done to a child. Jesus could have said almost anything to make the point. He chose the most violent metaphor available to Him.

The thief, He told us, comes only to steal and kill and destroy. When a child is harmed, all three are happening at once. Their innocence is stolen. Their developing self is killed. And the path back to the God who loves them is obstructed—not damned but blocked at the neurological level by the very wound that was inflicted on them. The wounding is not just an act against the child. It is an act against the relationship between that child and their Creator. It pushes them away from the only One who can fully hold them, and it does so before they have language to know what is being taken.

That is what we are talking about in this book. That is what is sitting in the pews. Not just sad histories. Not just unfortunate childhoods. Living evidence of what the enemy does when he gets his hands on a child.

I will not pretend to be neutral about it. I am not neutral about it. My brothers Adam and Patrick are dead because of it.

A Word to the Church

For 2,000 years, the church could honestly say it did not know. The neuroscience did not exist. The ACE research was not published until 1998. The mechanism by which a wound inflicted at age four becomes a heart attack at 54 was hidden from every generation of pastors that came before this one. Their silence was the silence of people who genuinely could not see.

That excuse is now expiring.

We know. The science is settled. The data is in. The pathway from wound to addiction to early death has been mapped with the kind of precision usually reserved for cancer pathways. And every pastor in America now has access to the same body of evidence that any first-year medical student does.

Which means that from this point forward, silence is no longer blindness. It is choice.

I want to be careful here, because I love the church, and I am writing this book *for* the church. I have spent years building a framework, a curriculum, and a certification program *to equip the church*—not to embarrass it. But love does not mean flattery, and the church needs to hear something most of us have been too polite to say out loud:

The American church has become very good at being comforting and has forgotten how to be fierce. We have remembered Jesus who blessed the children and forgotten Jesus who warned what would happen to anyone who harmed them. We have learned to host the wounded and forgotten how to fight for them. We have become a hospital that has misplaced its will to defend its patients.

Jesus made a whip. He cleared the temple. He called religious leaders who burdened wounded people *whitewashed tombs*. He was capable of pastoral tenderness and prophetic fire in the same afternoon—and He used both, because both were required. The wound in front of Him called for tenderness. The system that made the wound called for fire.

Childhood trauma is the largest unaddressed wound on the American church's pews, and the largest unspoken evil happening inside American homes. It is killing 1,401 of our neighbors every day. It is sitting in your sanctuary right now. And the call on the church is not to be sad about it, sympathetic toward it, or aware of it. The call is to stand up, see it clearly, name it as the evil it is, and become the institution God designed it to be: a place where the wounded actually heal and where the next generation of children is protected from being wounded in the first place.

That requires courage. Not crudeness. Not culture-war posturing. Real, costly, biblical courage—the kind that walks toward suffering instead of past it, that names sin without flinching, and that builds the structures necessary to defeat what it has named.

Every other institution in this country has had its reckoning with childhood trauma. The medical system. The justice system. The schools. The corporate world. The church is the last large institution in America that has not yet stood up and said: *This is evil, we are coming for it, and we will not be silent any longer.*

That silence ends with this generation of pastors. With the people who read this book and decide they are done managing the symptoms of a wound their congregations never named. The 2,000 years of blindness are over. What comes next is either courage or complicity. There is no middle category left.

I am writing this book because I believe the church will choose courage. I have staked the rest of my life on that bet.

What Could Be

But imagine this: churches that learn to see the bleeding. Churches that become structurally equipped to heal trauma—not just aware of it, not just sympathetic to it, but trained, certified, and proud to offer real help. Churches known not for what they're against but for what they heal. Where the most wounded people in your community discover that the safest place to get help is the church down the street, offering trauma-responsive care that addresses both the soul and the nervous system.

Not replacing faith with therapy. Not replacing prayer with science. Integrating them—the way God always intended. Because prayer is powerful. Faith matters. But the fractured bone still needs to be set.

This is what becomes possible when churches close what I call the Knowing-Doing Gap. That is the distance between what the world now understands about childhood trauma and what we are actually doing about it. It is the most dangerous gap in the trauma field today. We are rich in awareness. We are starving for action. The Knowing-Doing Gap is where 1,401 people disappear every single day.

Every church, every institution that touches human beings, sits somewhere on a four-level spectrum.

Level 1 is Trauma-Unaware: the wound is invisible and the only prescription is "try harder."

Level 2 is Trauma-Aware: the church knows the problem exists but has not changed how it operates.

Level 3 is Trauma-Informed: training has begun and language has shifted, but the focus remains on avoiding harm rather than creating healing.

Level 4 is Trauma-Responsive: the church has crossed the only line that matters—from knowing to doing, from managing the wound to closing it. Level 4 is the new gold standard. It is where Jesus's promise of rest for the weary is finally, truly delivered.

United Against Childhood Trauma (UACT) exists to close that gap. To move the church, and every institution that touches the lives of the wounded, from Level 3 to Level 4. From informed to responsive. From spiritual aspirin to setting the fractured bone.

That is what this book is about.

This Is Your Kairos Moment

The Greek word Kairos means "the appointed time." The critical moment when everything could change—when God's invitation and human readiness meet, when what has always been possible suddenly becomes urgent.

This is the church's Kairos moment. You can learn to see the bleeding. You can learn what healing requires. You can become the refuge trauma survivors have been desperately searching for.

Or you can keep doing what you've always done.

The gods were never angry. And the people sitting in your pews don't need to sacrifice more. They need you to see them, to understand what happened to them, and to create environments where healing is finally possible.

The sea doesn't part until someone steps into the water.

Before we go further, I need to address the question I know is already forming in your mind, because it formed in mine, and it wouldn't let me go until I found the answer. If God heals, why didn't prayer heal Shannon, Pastor Darren's wife? Why didn't it heal me? I spent five years trying to answer this question honestly. The full answer is in Chapter 7, but I'll share the short answer so you can read without that question blocking everything else:

Prayer does heal. It healed everything prayer was designed to heal. Shannon is alive today because of her faith—and by any biological measure, she should not be. What prayer couldn't do was repair the neurobiological damage that childhood trauma had inflicted on the physical structure of her brain. Not because prayer isn't powerful enough, but because that is not what prayer was designed to do. God designed the Gospel to heal the wound of separation from Him. He also designed the brain, and He placed in this generation the specific clinical tools to repair the wounds trauma created. Both provisions are from the same Creator. Both are required for complete healing. The church has been offering one and wondering why people aren't getting fully well.

This is not a book about the limits of faith. It is a book about the fullness of provision. And the invitation—for the first time in human history—to use both tools together.

Let's begin.

This book moves in five parts.

First, the invisible crisis—what's actually happening in the pews that churches can't see, and what it's costing us in lives, families, and faith.

Second, the theological blind spot—how 2,000 years of Christian tradition built powerful frameworks for spiritual problems but left the church completely unprepared for neurobiological wounds.

Third, the science the church needs—what childhood trauma actually does to the developing brain, why traumatized people can't "just forgive" or "just have more faith," and what healing actually requires.

Fourth, the path forward—what it means to become a trauma-responsive church, and how to start.

Fifth, the promise—what becomes possible when a church makes this journey, measured in lives changed, families healed, and communities transformed.

Each part builds on the one before it. By the end, you will be equipped to do three things you cannot do today: identify the signs of unresolved childhood trauma in the people sitting in your pews—not as a clinician, but as a shepherd who finally has eyes to see; design environments, language, and practices that stop re-wounding the wounded and start making healing possible; and make the case—to your board, your staff, your congregation, and yourself—for why a trauma-responsive church is not a theological compromise but the fullest expression of what the church was always called to be.

PART ONE

THE WOUND

Chapter One

The Invisible Wound

"The word 'trauma' comes from the Greek meaning 'wound,' and wounds bleed."

–Michael Menard

Shannon

She seemed blessed.

That's what everyone said about Shannon. Perfect wife for a pastor. Perfect partner for a man leading one of the fastest-growing evangelical churches in Middle Tennessee. Perfect smile. Perfect balance of warmth and competence. The kind of woman other women wanted to be, and men pointed their wives toward. She poured herself into the church in every way she knew how, showed up early on Sundays to make sure every detail was right, and stayed late to lock up. She had an eye for design and beauty, created spaces that reflected hospitality and love. When people saw Shannon, they saw someone who had it all together.

Shannon had a gift—she could see what was broken in others. What no one saw, including Shannon herself, was that something had been broken in her too: a wound that had been bleeding for as long as she could remember.

The Childhood That Shaped Her

Shannon was relocated often during her childhood. Her father's work was inconsistent, so the family never stayed anywhere long enough to put down roots. She counted it once; fifteen different homes by the time she was in high school. Different towns, different schools, always the new kid with no friends, always starting over. She learned early that nothing was permanent. That security was something other people had.

Her parents drank. Heavily, routinely, in the way that becomes the weather of a home—you don't notice it until you leave and feel what air without it tastes like. There were fights. Loud ones. Shannon remembers being seven years old, watching her mother throw her father's clothes onto the porch in the rain, load the kids into the car, and leave in the middle of the night. It happened more than once. The marriage was marked by her father's unfaithfulness and her mother's depression. A depression so pervasive that Shannon's mom slept most of the time, leaving nine-year-old Shannon with the weight of caring for her one-year-old brother.

Both parents carried pain of their own that was never treated and never talked about. They stopped drinking when Shannon was in sixth grade—an Assembly of God church got hold of them, they made a profession of faith, and the alcohol stopped. But the depression stayed. The emotional absence stayed. The silence stayed. They were never healed. They were just sober.

Shannon does not remember her parents talking to her, not really. Not about life, about feelings, about what was happening inside her. There were three children in that house, and all grew up in the same emotional desert—no one asking how they were, no one noticing what they felt, no one saying the words children need to survive. She rarely felt loved, rarely felt seen. She would describe it years later as growing up invisible.

And then there was what happened to her body.

Shannon was five years old the first time a child in the neighborhood violated her. She was a little girl who didn't know what was happening, only that it felt wrong and that she couldn't tell anyone. There were other incidents in the years that followed—more than one, more than one person, spread across her childhood like a pattern she had no power to stop. When she was sixteen, she was date raped.

She told no one.

Shannon was a "homely" kid by her own description—buck teeth, cat-eyeglasses, always the awkward new girl who didn't know the social codes of yet another school. Kids are brutally precise in finding what hurts. She was teased relentlessly. For years, she had almost no pictures taken of herself because she hated what she saw.

By the time Shannon reached her teenage years, her nervous system had been absorbing shock after shock for over a decade. She didn't have language for it. Nobody did. She just knew something inside her was broken in a way she couldn't fix, and she started doing what the body does when it can't find relief: she turned to whatever would numb the pain. In seventh and eighth grade, she drank until she blacked out. She stole things she didn't even want. Later, she cut herself—carving into her own skin trying to make the interior pain visible, trying to feel something she could control. She hit walls until she broke her hand on more than one occasion.

The church would have called what Shannon was doing sin. And by the letter of it, some of it was. But the Greek word in Galatians for restore—used when describing how believers should respond to someone *caught* in wrongdoing—is the same word ancient physicians used for setting a broken bone: *Katartizo.* Caught in wrongdoing. Trapped. Ensnared. Shannon wasn't choosing destruction. The wound had snared her. What she needed wasn't discipline. It was a physician who knew how to set bones.

The Faith That Kept Her Alive

In seventh grade, Shannon found the Lord. Or more precisely, the Lord found her, in a small Bible camp, in a life that hadn't given her much reason to hope. She wanted it with everything she had. She rededicated her life in ninth grade. She went to Bible school in Tulsa, chasing after the God who she believed could heal what she could not.

She prayed.

She read scripture.

She served.

She surrendered.

She did everything the faith said to do, with sincere conviction and real hunger for God.

The healing she was promised still did not come.

That is not to say Shannon's faith did nothing. I believe that her faith kept her alive during the years when staying alive was not a certain thing. The grace she had received, partially received through a neurobiologically wounded system, was still enough to create a floor. It kept her from the addiction spiral that swallowed others who carried her wound profile. She survived. That is not a small thing.

But surviving is not healing. And Shannon knew the difference.

She married Darren Tyler in Tulsa, where they both worked at the same restaurant. He was gifted and on fire for God, but he was also underemployed, with no guarantees he could provide the stability

Shannon had never experienced. For a woman who grew up watching her parents' marriage buckle under financial pressure and emotional chaos, it could easily have been history repeating itself. It wasn't salvation. It was a choice made on faith, in every sense of the word. They built a life together and eventually a church—Conduit Church in Franklin, Tennessee, which grew faster than either ever anticipated.

Shannon poured herself into it. She ran operations, managed volunteers, oversaw facilities, and organized community outreach among other responsibilities. For years she did the work of three staff members because there wasn't anyone else. She was asking for help but was not getting it. She was invisible again, seen simply as the pastor's wife, which was not a job description anyone had figured out.

She smiled. She showed up. She served.

She bled.

I want to name something before we go further, because it is easy to lose in a story about wounds. Shannon survived. She built a marriage, raised children, held a congregation, and kept showing up. That is not a footnote to her trauma. That is a list of resources—faith, work, loyalty, the capacity to tell the truth about herself—and she had them the entire time. Trauma is not the whole of anyone. When you look at the wounded people in your church, you are also looking at everything that has kept them alive so far. Find that, and you have found what you are building on.

The Body Starts Keeping Score

In 1995, Shannon was diagnosed with rheumatoid arthritis. She was in her early twenties. The immune system that was designed to protect her had turned against her, attacking her own joints, her own tissue, her own body. Physiological symptoms of an emotional wound. Doctors treated the symptoms, but no one asked what had happened to her as a child.

Nobody knew to ask.

Research now confirms what Shannon's body was demonstrating twenty years before she understood. Childhood trauma doesn't just wound the mind. It wounds the immune system. The chronic cortisol flooding that comes from years of living in survival mode creates sustained inflammation, which is one of the mechanisms behind autoimmune disease, heart disease, cancer, and dozens of other conditions that look like medical problems but are biological ones.

No doctor can prove what caused any one person's autoimmune disease, and I am not going to pretend otherwise. But we know what thirty years of stress hormones do to an immune system. And we know what Shannon's childhood did to her nervous system. Her body had been running emergency protocols since she was five years old. Something was going to give. By 2010, Shannon was decades into her silent suffering, but something shifted that year. She attended a two-weekend therapeutic intensive with Darren. It provided a structured environment where trained therapists and counselors spend time observing participants, listening to them, watching how they move through the world. At the beginning of the weekend, each participant was given a single word—a word the therapists believed captured something true and deep about that person's core wound.

Shannon's word?

Worthless.

She sat with that word. She didn't argue with it, because somewhere underneath all the competence and the service and the smile, she had always known it was there. That was the word that childhood had written on her—written on her body, written on her nervous system, written in the silence of parents who never told her she mattered, written in the violations of people who treated her as an object, written in the moves and the loneliness and the invisibility.

Worthless.

This was the first time anyone had named it. The first crack of light in forty years of darkness.

But knowing the name of your wound and knowing how to treat it are two different things. Shannon left the intensive with more self-awareness than she'd ever had. She still didn't know what to do with it.

The Book That Changed Everything

By 2015, Shannon's body was shutting down. The rheumatoid arthritis had progressed. A deep depression had settled in that wouldn't lift. She described that season in words that I have not been able to forget: "It felt like I was dying from loneliness and emotional abandonment."

Dying from loneliness. I want you to read that twice, because that is not a metaphor. That is a clinical description of what chronic emotional isolation does to the human body. Shannon's nervous system had been running on empty for decades, and the body was beginning to submit its final invoice.

It was during this season that a friend suggested an audiobook, *When the Body Says No* by Dr. Gabor Maté.

Shannon almost dismissed it. A book about the body's response to stress? She had enough to deal with without adding assigned reading to the list. But something made her listen.

Halfway through, she pulled over her car and sat in a parking lot and wept.

The book was describing her life. Every chapter. Every symptom. Every pattern. Gabor Maté, a physician who spent decades watching his patients die from stress-related diseases and asking why, was laying out the biological mechanism that connected childhood emotional experience to adult physical disease with a precision that felt like someone had been following Shannon around with a notepad since 1972.

What Shannon heard in that book, for the first time in her life, was this: There is a reason. Not a spiritual reason which required more faith. Not a personal failure that required more effort. A biological reason. A comprehensible, documented, scientifically validated reason why her body was doing what it was and why her soul felt the way it felt.

She described what happened next in a way that every person in your congregation needs to hear:

"It confirmed what I felt I had known for years—there was a deeper reason for the physical diseases and emotional battles I had been enduring for decades."

She had known. Somewhere in her body, in the place where the truth lives before the mind can catch up to it, she had always known. The book gave her permission to believe what she already felt.

And then, for the first time in her life, Shannon did something she had never done before.

She told a friend the truth.

Not all of it, not yet. But she began, carefully, haltingly, to speak out loud about the emotional battles she had been carrying alone. She had never really spoken about her life before that. Decades of silence—the silence she had learned as a child in a house where no one talked about anything—began to crack.

That crack was the beginning of everything.

And the breaking points, Shannon would tell you, did not always come from the obvious places. In 2018, her daughter Maddie got married. It should have been one of the greatest days of Shannon's life. Instead, it broke her. Not because anything went wrong—the day was beautiful—but her nervous system, running on decades of deficit, had no room left for joy. A system shaped by childhood trauma does not distinguish between a threat and an overwhelming moment of love. Both require more than Shannon had.

She shut down. And in the days and weeks that followed, she found herself quietly severing the connections associated with that day—friends who had been dear to her for years, people who had helped plan the wedding, relationships she had cherished. She stopped reaching out. She couldn't explain why. She just couldn't go back there. This is what a brain in chronic survival mode does when it finally hits its limit. It doesn't just shut down. It amputates, protecting itself the only way it knows how: Cutting away anything connected to the moment it could no longer carry.

The Floor

About twelve years ago, Shannon hit the bottom. Not metaphorically. Her body was giving out. The depression was so heavy she could barely move through it. She wasn't sleeping. She described it to me as a negative ten on a ten-point wellness scale—the place where you are one decision away from not being here anymore. She was that close to the edge. There were guns in the house. She didn't tell anyone why she didn't want them there, but she knew.

She would describe that season later in words that are almost unbearable to read.

"I felt numb. I had no words, no prayers. I couldn't read my Bible. I felt like I was merely existing in a shell."

The woman who had poured herself into the church for decades had nothing left. No language for God. No access to the faith that had always been her foundation. What remained was the most stripped-down version of holding on she could manage: she kept getting up. She kept serving others. She listened to worship music every day. One podcast—Joyce Meyer—because it was all her nervous system could absorb. She pressed into Jesus the only way she still could, not with words or scripture, but in the sheer, stubborn act of *not* stopping.

And still, she prayed. Still, she tried harder, believed more, served faithfully, submitted completely. Because that's what the church had always told her to do.

Three years ago, after a period of unsustainable pressure at the church she helped build—her voice unheard, her contributions unacknowledged, her pain invisible to the people closest to her—Shannon was formally diagnosed with major depression and PTSD. She could barely walk through the doors of the building. She took time away. She finally stopped trying to outrun what she was carrying.

And she started to heal.

Not overnight, not dramatically, but deliberately. She went to counseling—real, consistent, trauma-informed counseling—and stayed with it. She did kinesiology for two and a half years, working with her body the way she had never been allowed to as a child, learning that healing wasn't just a spiritual event, but a physical one. She filled her days with life-giving music, letting it reach the places words couldn't. She listened to audiobooks—the same way Gabor Maté's voice had found her in that parking lot years earlier, other voices now continued the work, speaking truth into a nervous system that was finally ready to receive it. For the first time in her life, Shannon wasn't just surviving, she was being treated.

And the difference, she would tell you, is everything.

What Her Body Was Trying to Tell Her

Here's what Shannon didn't know for nearly fifty years, what her church didn't know, what almost no one in the pews around her had any idea about:

What happened to Shannon as a child didn't just hurt her feelings, it rewired her brain. And it destroyed her body.

The human brain develops from the inside out and the bottom up. The lower brain structures—the amygdala, the brain's alarm system, the part that scans for danger and triggers the body's survival response—develop first. And they develop in direct response to the environment a child inhabits. When a child grows up in an environment of chronic unpredictability, emotional neglect, sexual violation, and fear, those lower brain structures are shaped by threat. The amygdala gets calibrated to a world where danger is always coming. It fires constantly; it doesn't know how to stop.

The cortisol and adrenaline that flood a child's body during ongoing trauma are not just temporary stress responses—they are literally sculpting the developing brain. The hippocampus, which is supposed to help file memories as "past" and regulate the body's fear response, shrinks under prolonged stress. The prefrontal cortex—the seat of reason, perspective, and emotional regulation—cannot fully come online when the lower brain is perpetually screaming danger. The body's accelerator gets stuck to the floor. The brake never fully engages.

And the immune system, as Gabor Maté documented and as Shannon's body demonstrated, it gets caught in the crossfire. Chronic cortisol flooding creates sustained inflammation. Sustained inflammation can trigger autoimmune responses. The body, designed to protect itself, begins attacking itself. Rheumatoid arthritis. Endometriosis. Multiple surgeries. A body that should have been thriving, slowly dismantling itself from the inside out.

Shannon's anxiety was not a spiritual problem. Her depression was not a faith failure. Her autoimmune disease was not bad luck. Her inability to feel the peace that others seemed to experience so easily was not evidence that God was distant or that she wasn't surrendered enough.

It was evidence of a nervous system that had been in survival mode since she was five years old. And a body that had been paying the bill for half a century.

The wound needed treatment. Not just comfort. Not just prayer. Treatment.

What Healing Actually Looks Like

Shannon began working with a therapist who specialized in trauma. She did counseling, kinesiology, life-giving music, audiobooks—layer by layer, she was treating what had never been treated. And then came the final missing piece: she started neurofeedback, a therapeutic process that helps retrain the dysregulated brain, teaching it to move out of the survival state it has been locked in for decades. From October 2025 to March 2026, just months before these words were published, something unlocked. The healthy pathways trauma had blocked for 50 years began to open. She began to understand, for the first time, why prayer alone hadn't healed her: The neurobiological wound had been blocking her capacity to fully receive what she was praying for. Now, finally, it wasn't.

The trauma wasn't evidence that God had abandoned her. It was a physical barrier—in her brain chemistry, her nervous system, the actual structure of her body—that was keeping grace from landing where she needed it most. She had received enough grace to survive. Now, with the wound finally being treated, she was beginning to receive the rest of it.

She didn't abandon her faith to heal. She combined it with science. Prayer *and* therapy. Scripture *and* neurofeedback. The God she had believed in since seventh grade *and* the clinical tools He had placed in the world for precisely this purpose.

The transformation has not been instant. Shannon would be the first to tell you that. It has been a journey—messy and nonlinear and sometimes brutal. There are still hard days. There are still layers being uncovered. She is not standing at the finish line looking back. She is still on the road.

But Shannon is no longer the woman who was bleeding invisibly in the front row of her husband's church. She is finding her voice for the first time in her life. She is discovering who she is when the wound isn't running everything. She is, slowly and with great courage, becoming whole.

When I asked Shannon if she was ready to let her story be told publicly, she said yes. Not because the healing is complete, but because she knows there are thousands, even millions of people sitting in pews right now who are exactly where she was. Suffering in silence. Praying harder. Trying to earn what can't be earned.

Dying from loneliness.

Bleeding on the inside while they smile on the outside.

Shannon's message to them is simple:

"*You're* not broken. You're wounded. And there is healing available that the church never knew to offer."

Here's something you need to understand, because it changes everything: The word "trauma" comes from the Greek word for wound. When ancient physicians used the word, they meant a spear through the chest, a broken bone, or a gash that bleeds—the kind of injury you can see, that requires immediate attention, that will kill you if left untreated.

Over time, we began applying the word to psychological wounds, but the original meaning holds—trauma is a wound, and just like physical wounds, psychological wounds bleed into our relationships, our health, our immune systems, our capacity to function, our ability to experience peace and joy and safety.

Shannon had been bleeding for nearly fifty years.

And here's the word for what is now happening to her. The word "healing" comes from the Old English hælan, meaning "to make whole." Same root as "holy" and "wholeness." They're not just similar—they're the same word, branching from the same ancient trunk. To heal is to become whole. To become whole is to approach holiness.

Not holiness as moral perfection, not holiness as sinlessness achieved through willpower, but holiness as God originally intended it: completeness, integration, being fully yourself, undivided, no longer at war with your own nervous system.

This is what trauma steals. It fractures us, splits us into pieces. The part that remembers and the part that can't stop running, the part that needs connection and the part that can't trust anyone, the part that believes God loves you and the part that is convinced you are worthless.

Worthless.

That was the word the therapists gave Shannon in 2010. That is the word that childhood trauma writes on a person's core identity. And that is precisely the wound that the Gospel of grace was designed to heal—if the channel is open to receive it.

Shannon is becoming whole. Without more sacrifice or trying that much harder, and instead, through healing that addresses the actual wound—body, mind, and spirit together. Exactly the way Jesus healed people. He didn't just comfort them. He made them whole.

The woman who had been bleeding for twelve years didn't just stop bleeding. She was restored to her community, released from shame, made whole in every dimension of her existence.

That's what healing really is. And that's what Shannon is finally finding by adding to it the one thing the church never knew to offer her: treatment for the wound.

Shannon is still at Conduit Church, still beside her husband, but now, she is *real*. Now when someone says, "I'm struggling," she doesn't offer a simple Bible verse and a promise to pray for them. She asks a different question:

"What happened to you?"

Not "What's wrong with you?"

Not "What are you doing wrong?"

"What happened to you?"

Because underneath every dysfunctional behavior, every mental health struggle, every autoimmune disease, every breakdown, every addiction, and every sleepless night is almost always a wound. Trauma. An adverse experience that rewired the developing brain and created patterns that look like character flaws, or spiritual failures, or just bad luck—but are actually injury responses.

Shannon's anxiety wasn't a spiritual problem. It was her amygdala, stuck in overdrive from the childhood that shaped her.

And she knows there are many more in her congregation who have been bleeding.

Here's what Shannon didn't know for nearly fifty years, and what most churches still don't know: Her story isn't unusual, it's the norm.

In 1998, the Centers for Disease Control and Kaiser Permanente published what would become one of the most important public health studies in history—the Adverse Childhood Experiences Study, or ACE

Study. It asked a simple question: What happened to you as a child, and how is it affecting your health now?

The answers changed everything we thought we knew about why people suffer.

One hundred and eighty million American adults—70% of the population—have experienced at least one adverse childhood experience. Not 70% of people in prison; not 70% of people in psychiatric hospitals. 70% of all Americans.

That means in any given congregation, most people sitting in the pews carry childhood trauma.

The majority.

And we don't see it. We don't ask about it. We don't have language for it. We don't have systems to address it.

In the next chapter, I'm going to show you exactly what those numbers look like—and what they're costing us in lives lost. But first, I want you to sit with what you just read. If you're a faith leader, think about your congregation. Think about the people you see every Sunday who look fine, but might be dying inside. Think about yourself and your family.

They're not spiritual failures.

They're not lacking faith.

They're wounded. And wounds bleed.

Chapter Two

Bleeding in the Pews

"The church isn't the villain of this story. The church is blind. And there's a difference."

–Michael Menard

Marcus

MARCUS LEFT.

He stayed for 15 years—longer than most who carry what he carried. He showed up faithfully, served in the youth ministry, gave generously, participated in small groups. He looked like the model Christian man: committed, stable, growing in faith.

What people didn't know: Marcus had survived childhood sexual abuse by a family member. Years of it. And the church—with its emphasis on forgiveness, on honoring parents, on not speaking ill of family, on trusting God to work all things for good—felt less like a sanctuary and more like another place where his pain had to stay hidden.

Every sermon about family values felt like a knife. Every Mother's Day and Father's Day celebration was agony. Every testimony about

God healing families made Marcus feel more alone, more defective, more certain that his family's brokenness disqualified him from the abundant life everyone else seemed to be experiencing.

He tried to talk about it once. In a small group. Carefully, vaguely, just testing whether there was room for his reality in this place.

"Have you forgiven them?" someone asked.

"Maybe God is working through this to make you stronger," another offered.

"All things work together for good," a third reminded him, kindly, from Romans 8:28.

Marcus never brought it up again.

He kept coming. Kept serving. Kept pretending. But something had broken in that moment—the realization that the church didn't have space for his story. That his trauma was too big, too ugly, too complicated for the neat theological boxes people wanted to put it in.

Marcus started therapy on his own. Found a trauma specialist who helped him understand that his anxiety, his difficulty with relationships, his constant hypervigilance—all of it made sense given what he'd endured. He wasn't spiritually deficient. He was injured.

The therapy helped. But it also made church harder. Because now Marcus could see the gap between what Jesus offered and what the church was delivering. Jesus saw wounded people and moved toward them. The church saw wounded people and handed them a self-help book and a small group curriculum.

After 15 years, Marcus left. Not because he lost his faith. Because he chose healing over performance. Because staying meant choosing to keep bleeding just to maintain the appearance of wholeness.

He still believes in God. Still prays. Still reads scripture. But he does it alone now. In therapy. With a few close friends who know his story and don't try to fix it with platitudes.

The church counted Marcus as a casualty of the culture. "Another one lost to the world."

The truth: Marcus wasn't lost. He was bleeding. And he finally realized the church couldn't see it.

The Numbers Behind the Bleeding

Marcus isn't an outlier. He's a data point in an epidemic so vast it's almost impossible to comprehend.

The ACE Study—the landmark research published in 1998 by the CDC and Kaiser Permanente—surveyed over 17,000 adults about 10 categories of adverse childhood experiences: physical abuse, sexual abuse, emotional abuse, physical neglect, emotional neglect, domestic violence, household substance abuse, household mental illness, parental separation or divorce, and having an incarcerated household member.

The findings were staggering. Not because childhood suffering was surprising, but because of what it predicted.

Each adverse childhood experience a person carries doesn't just add to their risk, it multiplies it. Someone with an ACE score of 4 or higher is 3.1 times more likely to suffer from depression and 9.5 times more likely to attempt suicide. They face dramatically increased risk of heart disease, cancer, diabetes, autoimmune disorders, chronic pain, and early death. The higher the ACE score, the shorter the lifespan.

And addiction? An ACE score of 5 or higher makes a person 11.3 times more likely to become an injection drug user. Not because they're morally weak. Because their nervous system is desperately seeking relief from pain that never stopped.

One hundred and eighty million American adults carry at least one ACE. Fifty million children are accumulating them right now. And every single day, 1,401 Americans die from the long-term health consequences of childhood trauma. That's more than car accidents. More than homicides. More than most things we mobilize resources to prevent.

This isn't a fringe issue affecting a few wounded souls. This is a massive public health crisis sitting in every congregation in the country.

The Exodus

And people are leaving because of it.

Church membership has fallen from 70% in 1999 to under 50% today. The "nones"—people claiming no religious affiliation—have doubled. Thousands of churches are closing every year. Among millennials and Gen Z, the exodus is even more pronounced.

There are many factors driving people away from institutional religion. But one of the biggest is this: wounded people came to church looking for healing and found only judgment. They tried to be honest about their struggles and were told to pray harder. They sought help and were given platitudes. They confessed their brokenness and were made to feel like their faith was deficient.

So they left. Like Marcus.

Not because they don't believe in God. But because they learned that healing happens outside the church, not inside it. That therapy works where prayer alone doesn't. That the secular world has more compassion for their wounds than the religious world does.

Here's what's hardest to hear: they're not entirely wrong. Not because prayer doesn't work or faith doesn't matter, but because the church has forgotten that psychological wounds are wounds. Real injuries that require real treatment.

If someone walked into your church bleeding from a gash on their arm, you wouldn't tell them to pray harder and wait for God to heal it. You'd get them to an emergency room. You'd understand that God often heals through physicians who know how to suture wounds.

But when someone walks into church bleeding from psychological trauma—anxiety, depression, addiction, suicidal thoughts—we hand them a Bible verse and wonder why they're not getting better.

The Question We're Not Asking

When someone shows up anxious, depressed, addicted, self-harming—when their marriage is failing, their kids are struggling, their life is falling apart—the church asks spiritual questions:

"Are you reading your Bible?"

"Are you praying enough?"

"Is there unconfessed sin?"

"Have you truly surrendered to God?"

All potentially valid questions. But they're not the first question.

The first question should be: "What happened to you?"

Because Marcus's inability to stay in church wasn't worldliness. It was trauma sensitivity to an environment that retraumatized him every time he walked through the door. His hypervigilance wasn't lack of faith. It was a nervous system that learned in childhood that the people closest to you are the ones who hurt you.

Marcus is one of 180 million.

Sit with that number. In a congregation of 200, roughly 140 of them carry at least one adverse childhood experience. Some carry four, five, six or more. Some are functioning well despite it. Some are barely holding on. Some have already left. Some are still there but stopped being real a long time ago.

They're not spiritual failures. They're not resistant to God's work. They're not casualties of the culture.

They're wounded. And no one ever asked what happened to them.

What Comes Next

Here's what gives me hope: Once you see the bleeding, you can't unsee it.

Once you understand that anxiety can be a trauma wound, you can't go back to prescribing prayer as the only treatment. Once you know that depression can have neurobiological roots, you can't keep offering spiritual disciplines as the sole remedy. Once you recognize that people aren't leaving because they're losing faith but because the church can't see their wounds—everything changes.

And that's what the rest of this book is for. To help you see what you've been missing. To show you the science behind childhood trauma so you understand what you're looking at. To reveal why the church's traditional tools, as sacred and powerful as they are, weren't designed for this kind of injury. And to show you what becomes possible when churches finally learn to see the wound and respond to it.

The invisible wound is about to become visible.

Everything that follows depends on whether you're willing to look.

CHAPTER THREE

The Science of Suffering

> "The Spirit of the Lord is on me, because He has anointed me to proclaim good news to the poor. He has sent me to bind up the brokenhearted, to proclaim freedom for the captives and release from darkness for the prisoners."
>
> –Isaiah 61:1 / Luke 4:18

BEFORE WE TALK ABOUT what the church should do about trauma, you need to understand what trauma actually is. Not theologically. Not metaphorically. Physically. What happens in the body and brain of a child when they experience abuse, neglect, or household dysfunction. And why those wounds don't just hurt—they kill.

If you're going to lead your church to become trauma-responsive, you need to know what you're responding to. This isn't optional knowledge. This is the foundation. You can't heal wounds you can't see, and you can't see them if you don't know what to look for.

So let's start with the basics.

One thing before we do. What follows are teaching models, not photographs. The brain does not actually have four settings, and no single region runs the whole person. Researchers argue about the mechanisms, and they should. These pictures are simplifications, and they are accurate enough to change how you pastor—which is what they are for. Read them the way you would read a diagram of the heart in a first-aid class. Close enough to act on. Not the whole truth.

The Bear in the Woods

Imagine you're walking through the woods. It's a beautiful day. Birds singing, sunlight filtering through the leaves, a light breeze. You're relaxed, maybe thinking about what you'll have for dinner, when suddenly—

A bear.

Eight hundred pounds of muscle and teeth, thirty feet away, and it's looking right at you.

What happens next is not a choice. Your body takes over. In milliseconds—faster than conscious thought—your brain's alarm system activates. The amygdala, a small almond-shaped structure deep in your brain, screams: DANGER! And your entire physiology shifts into survival mode.

Your heart rate spikes. Blood pressure surges. Adrenaline and cortisol flood your system. Blood rushes away from your digestive organs and toward your muscles—you don't need to digest lunch right now; you need to run or fight. Your pupils dilate. Your hearing sharpens. Non-essential functions shut down. Your immune system, your reproductive system, your capacity for complex reasoning—all temporarily suspended. Everything your body has is redirected toward one goal: survive the next 60 seconds.

This is the stress response. The fight-or-flight system. And it's a miracle of engineering.

For thousands of years, this system kept your ancestors alive. The ones who could mobilize fastest when the bear appeared were the ones who survived to pass on their genes. The ones who stayed calm and thoughtful? They got eaten. Natural selection favored the jumpy, the vigilant, the ones whose bodies could go from zero to survival mode in a heartbeat.

Here's the important part: this system was designed for short-term threats. The bear attacks or it doesn't. You escape or you don't. Either way, the crisis resolves in minutes. And once it's over, your body is supposed to return to baseline. Heart rate comes down. Stress hormones clear out. Digestion resumes. The alarm system stands down. You go back to thinking about dinner.

But what happens when the bear never leaves?

When the Bear Never Leaves

For a child growing up in an abusive home, the bear lives in the house.

Maybe the bear is a father who rages without warning. Maybe it's a mother whose depression makes her emotionally absent and unpredictable. Maybe it's the chaos of addiction—never knowing which parent will show up, the sober one or the drunk one. Maybe it's violence between parents, or sexual abuse by a relative, or the grinding instability of poverty and homelessness.

Whatever form it takes, the result is the same: a child's stress response system, designed for brief emergencies, gets activated day after day, month after month, year after year. The alarm that was supposed to ring for five minutes and then shut off? It never shuts off. The child lives in permanent emergency mode.

And this changes everything.

When a developing brain is marinated in stress hormones, it doesn't develop normally. The architecture of the brain literally changes. Neural pathways that should be building connections for learning, emotional regulation, trust, and attachment—they get hijacked by survival circuits instead. The brain becomes expert at detecting threats, scanning for danger, preparing for the next attack. But it never learns how to calm down, how to trust, how to feel safe.

Think about what this means. A child's brain is like wet cement—it takes the shape of whatever presses into it. For a child in a safe, stable home, that shape includes: *I am loved. The world is generally safe. I can trust adults. When I'm upset, someone will help me calm down. When I make mistakes, I won't be destroyed.*

But for a child living with the bear, the cement hardens around very different shapes: *I am not safe. I cannot trust anyone. When I'm upset, I'm on my own. Danger could come at any moment. I must always be vigilant.*

These aren't conscious beliefs. They're not decisions the child makes. They're the wiring of the nervous system itself. And once that cement hardens, it's extraordinarily difficult to reshape.

The Brain on Trauma

Let me get specific about what childhood trauma does to the developing brain. You need to understand this because it explains why traumatized people can't "just get over it" and why telling them to "pray harder" doesn't work.

The Amygdala: The Smoke Detector. The amygdala is the brain's alarm system. Its job is to detect threats and trigger the stress response. In a traumatized brain, the amygdala becomes hyperactive—stuck in the "on" position. It's like a smoke detector that goes off every time you make toast. The person lives in a constant state of low-grade alarm, always scanning for danger, always ready to react. This isn't anxiety as a character flaw. It's a smoke detector that got misaligned by years of actual fires.

The Prefrontal Cortex: The Thinking Brain. The prefrontal cortex is responsible for executive functions—planning, decision making, impulse control, emotional regulation. It's what makes us human rather than purely reactive animals. But the prefrontal cortex doesn't fully develop until our mid-twenties, and chronic stress during childhood impairs its development. Traumatized children often grow into adults with weakened capacity for emotional regulation, impulse control, and long-term planning. Not because they're lazy or undisciplined, but because the part of their brain responsible for these functions didn't develop properly.

The Hippocampus: The Memory Processor. The hippocampus helps process memories and place them in proper context—"This happened in the past," "It's over now," "I'm safe in the present." Chronic stress hormones actually shrink the hippocampus. This is why traumatic memories often feel current rather than past. The person isn't just remembering the trauma—they're reliving it. Their brain literally cannot file the memory away as "over." A sound, a smell, or a phrase can send someone right back to the worst moment of their childhood because their brain hasn't properly processed that the danger is gone.

The Nervous System: The Accelerator and the Brake. The autonomic nervous system has two branches. The sympathetic nervous system is the accelerator—it revs you up for action. The parasympathetic nervous system is the brake—it calms you down and returns you to rest. A healthy nervous system moves fluidly between these states: accelerate when there's danger, brake when it's safe. But a traumatized nervous system often loses access to the brake. The person is stuck with their foot on the gas, unable to downshift into calm. Or sometimes the system is so exhausted from chronic activation that it crashes into freeze—a shutdown state that looks like depression or dissociation.

Why "Pray Harder" Isn't Enough

Before I show you the science, I need to say something to the pastor.

What you are about to read is not an argument against prayer. It is not a case for replacing faith with therapy. It is not a suggestion that God is limited or that Scripture is insufficient. If you read it that way, you will have missed the most important theological claim in this book.

What you are about to read is an explanation of why a completely sufficient spiritual provision has not been producing complete healing—and why that is not a failure of the provision, it is the nature of the wound.

Consider this: God designed the heart. He also placed in the world the knowledge to perform open-heart surgery. When a believer has a blocked artery, we do not tell them that getting surgery means they lack faith. We understand God heals through means—through the knowledge He has placed in the world, administered by the hands He has trained. We do not see cardiology as competing with prayer. We see it as a channel through which God's healing flows for this specific injury.

The science that follows is not a threat to your faith, it is a gift from the Creator of the brain, placed in this moment in history, to complete what the church has always known how to start.

Now you can understand why the standard church prescriptions often fail for traumatized people.

"Just trust God." The person's hippocampus developed under chronic threat during critical developmental periods. Their brain, in that moment, cannot reliably distinguish between past danger and present safety. Trust isn't a decision they can make—it's a capacity that was injured.

"Have more faith." Their amygdala is firing constantly, flooding their system with stress hormones. Faith requires feeling safe enough to surrender control. Their nervous system is screaming that surrender means death. This isn't weak faith—it's a survival system doing exactly what it was designed to do.

"Just forgive." Their prefrontal cortex—the part of the brain that enables complex reasoning about abstract concepts like forgiveness—may be underdeveloped. And even if it isn't, forgiveness requires feeling safe, and they don't feel safe. You're asking them to do calculus when their brain is still stuck in basic survival arithmetic.

"Read your Bible more." Reading requires concentration. Concentration requires a calm nervous system. Their nervous system is in chronic fight-or-flight. The words swim on the page because their brain is too busy scanning for threats to process complex text.

"Just let go and let God." Letting go requires the ability to relax, to release vigilance, to trust that someone else will keep you safe. Their entire neural architecture was built around the lesson that letting go gets you hurt. You're asking them to override millions of years of evolution and decades of personal experience based on a slogan.

I'm not saying prayer doesn't matter. I'm not saying faith is irrelevant. I'm saying that for many traumatized people, these spiritual practices require capacities that trauma disrupted. It's like telling someone with a broken leg to just walk it off. Walking is good. Legs are designed to walk. But first you must set the bone.

For traumatized people, the bone that needs setting is their nervous system. And that usually requires specialized intervention that helps rewire the brain's threat detection system, calm the overactive amygdala, and teach the nervous system that safety is possible.

The Four F's: How Trauma Shows Up

When the stress response activates, the body has four basic options. Understanding these will help you recognize trauma responses in your congregation—responses that often get mislabeled as character flaws or spiritual failures.

Fight. The person is aggressive, combative, controlling. In church, this might look like the elder who has to win every argument, the volunteer who becomes hostile when criticized, the spouse who dominates through anger. We call it "anger issues" or "control problems." It's often a nervous system stuck in fight mode.

Flight. The person escapes, avoids, stays busy. In church, this is the person who can't sit still in worship, who volunteers for everything to avoid being alone with their thoughts, who changes the subject whenever conversations get deep. We call it "restlessness" or "avoidance." It's a nervous system that feels safest when running.

Freeze. The person shuts down, dissociates, goes numb. In church, this is the member who seems emotionally flat, who can't make decisions, who checks out during conversations. We call it "depression" or "apathy" or "laziness." It's often a nervous system that has collapsed into shutdown because fighting and fleeing didn't work.

Fawn. The person appeases, people-pleases, abandons their own needs to keep others happy. In church, this is the volunteer who can't say no, the spouse who enables destructive behavior to keep the peace, the member who agrees with everyone to avoid conflict. We call it "being a servant" or "having a gentle spirit." It's sometimes a survival strategy learned in childhood: if I make the dangerous person happy, maybe they won't hurt me.

None of these responses are choices in the normal sense. They're automatic, reflexive, driven by a nervous system that learned to survive a dangerous childhood. The person often doesn't know why they're doing it. They just know they've always been this way.

And here's what breaks my heart: we often reward some of these trauma responses in church while condemning others. The fawner who never says no, who serves until they collapse, who abandons their own needs to please everyone—we hold them up as models of Christian service. The fighter who challenges everything and can't submit to authority—we shame them as prideful and rebellious. But both responses come from the same place: a nervous system shaped by childhood trauma, doing its best to survive.

The Body Keeps the Score

Here's something else the church needs to understand: trauma doesn't just live in the mind. It lives in the body.

When the stress response is chronically activated, it damages physical health. Cortisol, the primary stress hormone, is meant for short-term emergencies. When it floods the system day after day, year after year, it causes real, measurable harm:

The immune system weakens. Traumatized people get sick more often and have higher rates of autoimmune disorders—lupus, rheumatoid arthritis, multiple sclerosis, fibromyalgia. The immune system is stuck in chronic inflammation mode, so it starts attacking the body itself.

Inflammation increases. Chronic inflammation is now understood to be a major driver of heart disease, diabetes, and cancer. A body that never leaves emergency mode is a body slowly destroying itself.

The cardiovascular system suffers. High blood pressure, heart disease, and stroke are all significantly more common in people with childhood trauma.

The gut breaks down. The digestive system is one of the first things the stress response shuts down—you don't need to digest food when you're running from a bear. But when the bear never leaves, the gut never fully recovers. This causes irritable bowel syndrome, chronic stomach pain, acid reflux, and inflammatory bowel disease. Trauma survivors show up in gastroenterologists' offices at dramatically higher rates. Many have been told for years that their symptoms are "stress-related" or "all in their head." They're not. They're in their nervous system.

Chronic pain takes root. Headaches that won't resolve. Back pain with no structural cause. Jaw tension from years of clenching. Muscle tightness that no amount of stretching releases. The body is literally bracing for impact—holding itself in a defensive posture against a threat that ended years ago but the nervous system never got the message.

The brain itself changes. We've already talked about this, but it bears repeating: chronic stress hormones cause measurable changes in brain structure and function.

Think about the people in your congregation. The woman with fibromyalgia who's seen 12 doctors and none of them can explain why she hurts everywhere. The man with chronic GI problems who's had every test and nothing comes back positive. The volunteer with tension headaches so severe she misses church twice a month. The elder with unexplained chest pain that cardiologists can't account for.

What if the explanation isn't medical? What if it's biographical? What if the question isn't "What's wrong with your body?" but "What happened to you as a child?"

This is why the landmark ACE Study found that childhood trauma predicts virtually every major cause of death. Heart disease. Cancer. Stroke. Diabetes. Suicide. Liver disease. Chronic lung disease. The connection isn't mysterious or metaphorical. It's biological. Trauma damages bodies.

This is also why traumatized people often can't "think" their way to healing. The trauma isn't stored in their thoughts—it's stored in their nervous system, their muscles, their gut. They can understand intellectually that they're safe now, that the abuser is gone, that the danger is past. But their body doesn't believe it. Their body is still living in the past, still responding to threats that ended decades ago.

Dr. Bessel van der Kolk, one of the world's leading trauma researchers, titled his groundbreaking book *The Body Keeps the Score* for exactly this reason. The body remembers what the mind tries to forget. And until that body-level memory is addressed, healing remains incomplete.

Jamie

Let me tell you about my brother Jamie. His story is what all this science looks like in a real life.

Jamie is a man of deep, authentic faith. His relationship with God is real, personal, and unwavering. He knows Scripture, has served faithfully in multiple ministries, and trusts completely in God's power. Yet for 30 years, Jamie lived with a persistent undercurrent of depression and anxiety that never quite went away.

It wasn't debilitating. Jamie functioned well—built a successful career, raised a family, led Bible studies, prayed beautiful prayers that moved others to tears. From the outside, no one would have known anything was wrong. But Jamie knew. Something was off. A low-grade heaviness that colored everything. An anxiousness that never fully lifted. He could manage it, push through it, live with it—but it was always there, like background noise he'd learned to ignore but could never quite silence.

He did what faithful people do. He prayed. He claimed promises. He memorized verses about peace and joy. He asked elders for prayer. He never stopped believing God could heal him. The church offered him everything it knew how to give.

The medical route proved equally frustrating. Doctor after doctor prescribed medication after medication, but nothing seemed to address what was actually wrong.

Now you know why. Jamie's amygdala—his smoke detector—had been misaligned since childhood. His nervous system had lost access to the brake. His body was carrying decades of unprocessed stress in ways that no amount of prayer or medication could reach, because neither was designed to rewire a traumatized nervous system.

Then I started researching childhood trauma for a memoir about our shared upbringing. As I shared what I was learning, Jamie began to wonder: could his lifelong struggle be connected to what happened in our childhood? Not a spiritual failure, but a neurobiological wound?

He found a Christian therapist who specialized in trauma recovery and began EMDR therapy—Eye Movement Desensitization and Reprocessing. EMDR helps the brain finally process traumatic memories that have been stuck in the nervous system, moving them from "this is happening right now" to "this happened in the past and it's over."

After just seven sessions, Jamie experienced dramatic improvement. Not a magical cure—healing is rarely that simple—but a breakthrough that thirty years of prayer and medication hadn't produced. The persistent heaviness began to lift. The anxiety that had shadowed him for decades lost its grip. For the first time, Jamie felt like he was actually healing, not just coping.

Seven sessions. After thirty years.

Not because prayer failed him. Not because his faith was insufficient. But because the wound was neurobiological, and it needed neurobiological treatment. Prayer had been sustaining him. Faith had been keeping him alive. But the bone still needed to be set. And once it was, the healing that prayer and faith had been preparing him for could finally take hold.

Today, Jamie is thriving. He's become an outspoken advocate for therapy within the church, wanting others to know what he didn't know for three decades: that childhood trauma creates real wounds in the brain, and those wounds often need specialized care to heal—care that complements faith rather than replacing it.

Jamie's story is what inspired me to write this book.

His story reveals the gap: the church is equipped to address spiritual struggles but often blind to neurobiological ones. How many years might have been different if just one person in our church had understood how childhood trauma affects the brain?

How many more Jamies are sitting in your sanctuaries right now, faithfully praying, quietly struggling, waiting for someone to help them see what's actually wrong?

What Healing Requires

So, what actually heals trauma?

First, safety. Real, felt safety—not just intellectual safety. The nervous system needs to learn, at a visceral level, that danger is no longer present.

This can't be rushed. It can't be achieved by telling someone they should feel safe. It happens through consistent, predictable, trustworthy relationships over time.

Second, regulation. The nervous system needs to learn how to calm down—how to find the brake pedal. This often happens through "co-regulation": being with someone whose nervous system is calm helps your nervous system learn to be calm. This is why therapy relationships matter so much. It's also why church communities could be incredibly healing—if they knew how to provide a calm, regulated presence instead of anxious exhortations to try harder.

Third, processing. The traumatic memories stuck in the body need to be processed and integrated. This is the work of trauma-focused therapies like EMDR, Somatic Experiencing, and others. These approaches help the brain finally file the traumatic memories as "past"—completed events that are over now, rather than ongoing threats. This is exactly what happened for Jamie in those seven sessions.

Fourth, connection. Trauma happens in relationship, and it heals in relationship. Isolated healing isn't real healing. The person needs to experience safe, trustworthy relationships that contradict the lessons trauma taught: that people are dangerous, that trust leads to pain, that you're on your own. This is where the church could play an enormous role—if it understood what traumatized people actually need.

Notice what's not on this list. Trying harder. Believing more. Praying until the trauma goes away. Confessing whatever sin must be causing this.

These spiritual practices have their place. But they are not, by themselves, sufficient to heal neurobiological injury. And when we offer them as the only solution, we set traumatized people up to fail—and then to blame themselves for failing.

The Good News

Here's what I want you to hold onto: The brain can change.

Neuroscientists call it neuroplasticity—the brain's ability to rewire itself throughout life. The damage caused by childhood trauma is real, but it's not permanent. New neural pathways can be built. Hyperactive amygdalae can calm down. Nervous systems can learn to find the brake. It's not easy. It's not quick. But it's possible.

This is, in many ways, the scientific confirmation of what the gospel has always promised: healing is possible. Restoration is real. What was broken can be made whole.

But the healing often requires more than the church has traditionally offered. It requires understanding that we're dealing with neurobiological injury, not just spiritual failure. It requires patience measured in months and years, not weeks. It requires partnerships with mental health professionals who understand trauma. It requires creating environments of genuine safety, not environments of performance and judgment.

And it requires the church to do something it hasn't done well: to see people's pain without rushing to fix it, to sit with suffering without offering platitudes, to accept that some wounds take a long time to heal and that's not evidence of insufficient faith.

The science of suffering isn't meant to discourage you. It's meant to equip you. When you understand what trauma actually does to the brain and body, you can finally stop asking the wrong questions ("Why can't they just get over it?") and start asking the right ones ("What do they need in order to heal?").

The bear that never leaves can finally be chased away. The nervous system that never learned to rest can finally find peace. The brain that was shaped by danger can be reshaped by safety.

That's the promise. And the church—if it's willing to learn—can be part of making that promise real.

In the next chapter, we'll look at what happens when trauma goes unaddressed across a lifetime—and across an entire population. The disintegration of body, mind, relationships, and spirit. The true cost of the epidemic hiding in plain sight.

CHAPTER FOUR

The Total Disintegration

> "The effects of unresolved trauma can be devastating. It can affect our habits and outlook on life, leading to addictions and poor decision-making. It can take a toll on our family life and interpersonal relationships. It can trigger real physical pain, symptoms, and disease. And it can lead to a range of self-destructive behaviors."
>
> –Peter A. Levine, PhD[1]

I WANT TO SHOW you something that will change how you see your congregation forever.

Imagine a typical Sunday morning. Two thousand people file into a large evangelical church—families with children, young professionals, retirees, college students. They greet each other warmly, find their seats, sing worship songs, listen to the sermon. From the outside, it looks like a healthy, thriving community of faith.

But if you could see beneath the surface—if you could perceive the invisible wounds each person carries—you would witness something devastating. Not a spiritual crisis. A trauma crisis.

Based on the CDC-Kaiser ACE Study, here's what we know about any gathering of 2,000 American adults: only 600 experienced no adverse childhood experiences. That's 30%. Less than a third of your congregation grew up in homes free from abuse, neglect, or serious household dysfunction.[2]

The other 1,400 (70%) carry at least one ACE. And 420 of them—more than one in five—carry four or more, placing them at dramatically elevated risk for virtually every major health condition. Within that group, 144 people carry six or more ACEs and will die, on average, 20 years before their time.[3]

Those numbers are staggering enough on their own. But what they don't tell you is what the disintegration actually looks like—how it unfolds across every dimension of a person's life, compounding year after year, until the person who walks into your church on Sunday morning is barely holding it together.

Let me show you what I mean.

Angela

Angela didn't leave the church. She just stopped being real.

She's still there every Sunday. Still sings the worship songs. Still tithes. Still shows up for the occasional church event. But the real Angela—the one struggling with an eating disorder rooted in childhood emotional neglect, the one battling depression so severe she sometimes can't get out of bed, the one who's had three suicide plans in the last two years—doesn't come to church anymore.

Only the performance shows up. The mask. The version of Angela that people expect to see.

Angela's mother wasn't abusive in the way most people picture it. She didn't hit. She didn't scream. She just wasn't there—emotionally absent, unreachable, a ghost in her own home. Angela learned early on that her feelings didn't matter, that needing comfort was a burden, that she was fundamentally on her own in the world.

That lesson didn't stay in her childhood. It followed her into every dimension of her adult life—her body, her mind, her relationships, her faith. What happened to Angela as a child didn't just hurt her once. It's been disintegrating her for decades.

And Angela is not unusual. She's a data point in an epidemic. Her story is the story of the 1,400 people in your congregation who carry childhood trauma, playing out differently in each life but following the same devastating pattern.

The Physical Disintegration

Angela's eating disorder isn't about food. It isn't about vanity or self-control. It's about a nervous system that learned early on that the world is unsafe and the only thing she can control is what goes into her body.

Remember what we learned in the last chapter: when the stress response is chronically activated in childhood, cortisol floods the developing body day after day, year after year. That cortisol was designed for brief emergencies—run from the bear, then return to baseline. But when the bear never leaves, the cortisol never stops. And chronic cortisol exposure does measurable, predictable damage.

It weakens the immune system, leading to autoimmune disorders. It drives chronic inflammation, which is now understood to be a major factor in heart disease, diabetes, and cancer. It disrupts metabolic processes. It damages the cardiovascular system. The stress response that saved the child's life in the short term slowly destroys their body over the long term.

This is why the ACE Study found such stunning physical health outcomes. Among those 420 people in your congregation with four or more ACEs, approximately 24 will develop heart disease, 17 will suffer a stroke, 45 will develop liver disease, and 37 will develop chronic bronchitis or emphysema—at rates ranging from one and a half to more than three times those of people without childhood trauma.[4]

These aren't random misfortunes. They're the predictable consequences of what those people experienced as children. The wounds became embedded in their flesh.

Angela's body is keeping score. Her eating disorder has compromised her digestive system, her bone density, her heart. She's 38 and her body is functioning like someone 20 years older. Not because she's made bad choices. Because her nervous system has been running a survival program since she was six years old, and the body can only take so much.

And those 144 congregants with six or more ACEs? They represent roughly 2,880 total years of life that will be lost. Years they won't spend with their grandchildren. Years of service they won't offer. Gone. Because of what happened to them before they turned 18.

The Mental Disintegration

Angela has clinical depression. Not occasional sadness—the kind that makes getting out of bed feel impossible. The kind that drains color from the world and whispers that nothing will ever get better.

Here's why. Remember the prefrontal cortex—the thinking brain we discussed in the last chapter? It's responsible for emotional regulation, impulse control, and the ability to imagine a future different from the present. Chronic childhood stress impairs its development. And remember the hippocampus—the memory processor that helps distinguish past from present? Chronic cortisol shrinks it. Angela's brain was literally shaped by neglect into a structure that defaults to hopelessness, because the part that could regulate her emotions and the part that could file painful experiences as "over" were both disrupted during the years they were supposed to be developing.

She's not depressed because her faith is weak. She's depressed because childhood trauma altered her brain chemistry.

And she's not alone in your congregation. Among those with four or more ACEs, depression occurs at 3.1 times the rate of those without childhood trauma.[5] In a congregation of 2,000, that translates to roughly 232 people battling clinical depression—most of them silently.

But here's the number that should stop you cold: 80 people in your congregation have attempted suicide or will attempt it. Those with four or more ACEs are 9.5 times more likely to make that attempt.[6]

9.5 times.

Angela has had three suicide plans in the last two years. She has never told anyone at church. She sings worship songs on Sunday mornings with an exit strategy in her back pocket, and nobody knows because nobody asks. She's one bad week away from becoming a statistic—and the church would be stunned, because Angela always seemed fine.

The Social Disintegration

When people ask Angela "How are you?" she says "Blessed." When her small group shares prayer requests, she mentions work stress or car trouble—safe, manageable problems. The real stuff stays hidden.

This is what attachment disruption looks like in adulthood. A child who grows up with an emotionally absent parent learns that relationships are one-directional. You perform, they stay. You need something, they disappear. Vulnerability is dangerous. Intimacy is a setup for abandonment. These lessons get encoded into the nervous system itself, becoming automatic patterns that persist decades after the original neglect.[7]

Angela tried once to be honest. She mentioned to a woman in her small group that she was struggling with some "food issues." The woman recommended a Christian diet book and suggested they pray together about self-control.

That was the last time Angela said anything real.

The data confirms what Angela's story illustrates. Among those 420 high-ACE congregants, approximately 27 have been married three or more times—10.8 times the rate of those without childhood trauma.[8] Not because they're frivolous about marriage. Because their nervous systems are wired for threat detection, not intimacy. They either flee at the first sign of conflict or escalate every disagreement into warfare because they learned as children that staying too long gets you hurt.

And 135 of those high-ACE congregants—mostly women—were raped as adults, which is 7.1 times the baseline rate.[9] This isn't coincidence. Children who experience abuse often develop patterns that make them vulnerable to revictimization: difficulty reading dangerous situations, learned helplessness, attraction to relationships that replicate familiar dynamics. The trauma doesn't just stay in the past. It sets them up for more trauma in the future.

And then there's the intergenerational transmission. Parents who haven't healed from their own childhood wounds often—unconsciously, unintentionally—pass those wounds to their children. A dysregulated nervous system in a parent creates a chaotic environment for kids. In your congregation right now, there are children being raised by parents whose best is compromised by unhealed trauma. Those children will fill the next generation of pews carrying new versions of the same old wounds.

The Spiritual Disintegration

Angela still goes to church. She still believes in God—at least intellectually. But her relationship with God feels like her relationship with everyone else: a performance. She shows up. She goes through the motions. She doesn't show God the real her, because she learned at age six that the real her wasn't worth seeing.

This is the cruelest dimension of trauma's disintegration, and the one the church most needs to understand.

Think about what faith requires. Trust. Surrender. Believing that a powerful being you cannot see has your best interests at heart. Accepting that you are loved. Resting in the assurance that someone is watching over you.

Now think about what childhood trauma teaches. Don't trust anyone. Never surrender—surrender gets you hurt. Powerful beings who claim to care about you are liars. You are fundamentally unlovable.

The neural pathways are the problem. Remember the amygdala—the brain's smoke detector? In a traumatized person, it fires alarm signals every time they're asked to trust a Father they cannot see. Especially if the last father they trusted was the one who hurt them. Or the last mother they needed was the one who disappeared. Their nervous system has learned that authority figures are dangerous and surrender is death. Asking them to "let go and let God" triggers the same survival response as asking them to walk off a cliff.

McKinsey surveyed 41,000 people across 26 countries and found that spiritual health tracks with every other dimension of health. People reporting poor spiritual health were roughly four times less likely to report good mental health, and about half as likely to report good physical or social health.[10] Meaning is not decoration on a life. It is load bearing.

But here's the tragic irony: childhood trauma damages the very capacity that could help people heal. The person who most needs the comfort of faith is neurologically impaired in their ability to access it.

Angela can recite scripture. She can pray the words. But she can't feel God's presence because her nervous system won't let her guard down long enough to receive it. This isn't spiritual laziness. It's neurological blockage. The doorway to God that opens easily for others has been barricaded by years of survival programming.

The Addiction Crisis

Before we leave this portrait of disintegration, we need to talk about what happens when people can't bear the pain anymore.

Among those 420 high-ACE congregants, 68 are or will become alcoholics (5.3 times the baseline rate) and 14 have used or will use intravenous drugs (11.3 times the baseline rate).[11]

I need you to understand something crucial: addiction is not the problem. Addiction is the solution—a desperate, destructive, ultimately fatal solution, but a solution nonetheless. People don't become addicts because they lack willpower or moral fiber. They become addicts because they're in unbearable pain and the substance provides temporary relief.

The child whose nervous system was marinated in stress hormones for years discovers that alcohol calms the internal chaos. The teenager who was sexually abused finds that opioids make the memories bearable. The adult whose body holds decades of unprocessed trauma learns that certain behaviors—shopping, eating, sex, gambling, or work—provide momentary escape from feelings that would otherwise be overwhelming.

Dr. Gabor Maté, one of the world's leading experts on addiction, puts it simply: "The question is not 'Why the addiction?' but 'Why the pain?'"[12]

My brothers Patrick and Adam died from heroin overdoses. For years, I thought they were weak. I thought they made bad choices. I thought if they'd just tried harder, had more faith, found the right program, they'd still be alive.

I was wrong. They weren't weak. Their pain was greater than their hope. And the church—our church, the church they grew up in—never saw the wound beneath the addiction. Never asked what happened to them. Never understood that the heroin wasn't the problem. The heroin was how they survived the problem as long as they did.

The church has historically treated addiction as a moral failure requiring repentance and willpower. But the data is clear: addiction is far more often a trauma response than a moral failure. People don't need more shame. They need trauma healing. Without addressing the underlying wound, all the accountability groups and 12-step programs in the world will only produce white-knuckle sobriety at best—and relapse at worst.

The Total Picture

Angela sits in the third row of her church every Sunday carrying all four dimensions of disintegration at once. Her body is breaking down from an eating disorder rooted in childhood neglect. Her mind is battling depression and suicidal ideation driven by neurological damage she didn't choose. Her relationships are hollow performances because her nervous system learned that vulnerability means abandonment. And her faith—the one thing that might multiply her healing—is blocked by the very wounds that make healing necessary.

She is not an outlier. She is the norm.

And the church thinks it still has her. It doesn't. It has a ghost. The real Angela is somewhere else—in a therapist's office, in an eating disorder support group, in treatment programs the church doesn't know about—doing the real work of healing while the church goes on around her, oblivious.

The church sees attendance numbers and giving levels and volunteer sign-ups. It sees people who show up and sing and shake hands and say they're "blessed." It sees the performance of wholeness, not the reality of woundedness.

What This Means for the Church

Here's what I need you to understand: 70%. That's not a fringe population. That's not a specialized ministry for a particularly wounded few. That's the majority of every congregation in America.

The church has been operating on the assumption that most people are basically healthy, and a few are wounded. The data shows the opposite: most people are wounded and a few are basically healthy. We've had it exactly backward.

And that changes everything about how you do ministry.

It changes how you preach.

When 70% of your congregation has a dysregulated nervous system, every word you say is being filtered through a threat-detection lens. Language about God's anger, about judgment, about the cost of disobedience—it doesn't land the way you intend. For someone whose amygdala is already in overdrive, a sermon on God's wrath doesn't create holy reverence. It triggers a survival response. Their body floods with cortisol, their hearing narrows, and they spend the rest of the service in fight-or-flight, absorbing nothing. Meanwhile, language about safety, about God's delight in them, about being seen and known—that's what begins to calm the smoke detector. That's what opens the door to actual transformation. This doesn't mean you water down truth. It means you learn to deliver truth in a way that traumatized nervous systems can actually receive.

It changes how you design small groups.

Most small group curricula assume participants can be vulnerable on demand. Share your struggles. Confess your sins. Open up to people you've known for three weeks. For someone with a healthy attachment system, this might feel uncomfortable but doable. For someone whose nervous system learned in childhood that vulnerability gets you hurt, it's terrifying. It feels physically dangerous. And when they can't do it—when they freeze or deflect or give a surface-level answer—the group reads it as disengagement or spiritual immaturity. It's neither. It's self-protection. Trauma-responsive small groups build safety first. They earn trust over months, not minutes. They create predictable rhythms. They let people participate at the edges before asking them to move to the center. They understand that silence isn't resistance—it might be the bravest thing a traumatized person can do in a room full of strangers.

It changes how you counsel.

When someone comes to you in crisis—anxious, depressed, addicted, marriage falling apart—the first question shouldn't be: "Are you reading your Bible?" or "Is there unconfessed sin?" The first question should be: "What happened to you?" Not every struggle is rooted in trauma. But statistically, most are. And if you start with spiritual prescriptions for a neurobiological wound, you'll lose them—either because they leave in frustration, or because they stay and conclude that their inability to heal through prayer means God has abandoned them. A trauma-responsive pastor learns to recognize when a problem is spiritual and when it's neurobiological and knows when to treat and when to refer. This isn't admitting defeat. It's the same wisdom that sends a parishioner to an oncologist instead of trying to pray away cancer.

It changes how you handle church discipline.

The member who can't seem to stop the destructive behavior. The volunteer who keeps blowing up at people. The spouse who can't stay faithful. The parent who can't control their anger. Traditional church discipline assumes these are character problems requiring accountability and correction. And sometimes they are. But often—very often—they're trauma responses. The person isn't choosing destructive behavior. Their nervous system is driving it, running survival programs written in childhood that they may not even be aware of. Discipline without healing just adds shame to injury. It confirms what the traumatized person already believes: that they're fundamentally broken and beyond help. A trauma-responsive church learns to hold both accountability and compassion—to address the behavior while also addressing the wound that's driving it.

Until we flip our assumptions—until we start with the recognition that trauma is the norm, not the exception—we will continue to offer ministry that works for the minority and fails the majority.

In the next chapter, we'll look at the body count. The 1,401 people dying every day from the long-term health consequences of childhood trauma. The epidemic hiding in plain sight—and why the church needs to recognize this as the public health crisis it is.

But for now, I want you to sit with what you've just learned. Picture your congregation. Picture Angela in the third row. And know that behind the faces you see every Sunday, in bodies and minds and nervous systems you cannot see, the disintegration is happening. Physical. Mental. Social. Spiritual. Total.

They're bleeding in the pews. They have been for years.

The church thinks it still has them. It doesn't. It has their ghosts.

Will you be the one who learns to see the real person behind the mask?

Endnotes

1. Peter A. Levine, *In an Unspoken Voice: How the Body Releases Trauma and Restores Goodness* (Berkeley: North Atlantic Books, 2010).

2. V. J. Felitti, R. F. Anda, D. Nordenberg, et al., "Relationship of Childhood Abuse and Household Dysfunction to Many of the Leading Causes of Death in Adults: The Adverse Childhood Experiences (ACE) Study," *American Journal of Preventive Medicine* 14, no. 4 (1998): 245–258.

3. D. W. Brown, R. F. Anda, H. Tiemeier, et al., "Adverse Childhood Experiences and the Risk of Premature Mortality," *American Journal of Preventive Medicine* 37, no. 5 (2009): 389–396.

4. Felitti et al., "Relationship of Childhood Abuse," 245–258. Health outcome prevalence rates for 0 ACEs vs 4+ ACEs populations. Heart disease: 1.5x; Stroke: 1.6x; Chronic bronchitis: 3.1x.

5. Felitti et al., "Relationship of Childhood Abuse," 245–258. Depression prevalence: 18% for 0 ACEs vs 55% for 4+ ACEs (3.1x multiplier).

6. Felitti et al., "Relationship of Childhood Abuse," 245–258. Suicide attempt prevalence: 2% for 0 ACEs vs 19% for 4+ ACEs (9.5x multiplier).

7. R. F. Anda, V. J. Felitti, J. D. Bremner, et al., "The Enduring Effects of Abuse and Related Adverse Experiences in Childhood:

A Convergence of Evidence from Neurobiology and Epidemiology," *European Archives of Psychiatry and Clinical Neuroscience* 256, no. 3 (2006): 174–186.

8. Felitti et al., "Relationship of Childhood Abuse," 245–258. Three or more marriages: 0.6% for 0 ACEs vs 6.5% for 4+ ACEs (10.8x multiplier).

9. Felitti et al., "Relationship of Childhood Abuse," 245–258. Raped as adult: 4.5% for 0 ACEs vs 32% for 4+ ACEs (7.1x multiplier).

10. Erica Coe, Kana Enomoto, Jacqueline Brassey, and Victoria Bennett, "In Search of Self and Something Bigger: A Spiritual Health Exploration," McKinsey Health Institute, May 13, 2024, https://www.mckinsey.com/mhi/our-insights/in-search-of-self-and-something-bigger-a-spiritual-health-exploration

11. Felitti et al., "Relationship of Childhood Abuse," 245–258. Alcoholism: 3% for 0 ACEs vs 16% for 4+ ACEs (5.3x multiplier); IV drug use: 0.3% for 0 ACEs vs 3.4% for 4+ ACEs (11.3x multiplier).

12. Gabor Maté, *In the Realm of Hungry Ghosts: Close Encounters with Addiction* (Berkeley: North Atlantic Books, 2010).

CHAPTER FIVE

The Bodies We've Been Counting Wrong

"We have met the enemy and he is us."

–Walt Kelly, Pogo

EVERY YEAR, THE CENTERS for Disease Control publishes the leading causes of death in America.[1] You've probably seen the list. Heart disease at the top—around 700,000 deaths per year. Then cancer. Then COVID, or accidents, depending on the year. Stroke. Chronic respiratory disease. Alzheimer's. Diabetes.

We mobilize billions of dollars to fight these killers. We fund research. We launch awareness campaigns. We build hospitals and train specialists and develop medications. We treat these causes of death as urgent public health priorities—because they are.

But what if I told you we've been counting wrong?

What if the leading cause of death in America isn't on the CDC's list at all—because we've been categorizing the symptoms instead of the source?

What if something is killing more Americans than heart disease, more than cancer, more than anything else we track—and we've been looking right past it for decades?

The Number That Should Stop You Cold

1,401

That's how many Americans die every single day from causes directly attributable to childhood trauma.[2]

Not indirectly. Not loosely connected. Directly attributable—through rigorous epidemiological research that traces the causal pathways from adverse childhood experiences to adult mortality.

1,401 deaths per day.

511,365 deaths per year.

More than heart disease. More than cancer. More than strokes, accidents, Alzheimer's, and diabetes combined.

Childhood trauma is the number one cause of death in America.

Not number three, as I originally calculated when I began this research. Number one. When you properly attribute deaths to their root cause rather than their proximate mechanism, childhood trauma kills more Americans than anything else.

Let me show you how we know this.

The Mathematics of Misattribution

When someone dies of heart disease, the death certificate lists heart disease as the cause. When someone dies of liver failure, we count it as a liver death. When someone dies of a drug overdose, we add it to the overdose statistics.

But this is like saying someone died of "bullet wound" without asking who fired the gun.

The ACE Study and subsequent research have established clear, measurable, dose-dependent relationships between childhood trauma and virtually every major cause of death.[3] People with high ACE scores don't just have slightly elevated risks. They have dramatically elevated risks—200%, 300%, 500% higher than those without childhood trauma, depending on the condition.[4]

When you apply these risk multipliers to actual mortality data, a devastating picture emerges.

Take heart disease, the official "leading cause of death." The ACE Study found that people with four or more ACEs have 1.5 times the risk of ischemic heart disease compared to those with no ACEs.[5] When you calculate how many of those 700,000 annual heart disease deaths are attributable to the elevated risk caused by childhood trauma, you get a significant portion of that total.

Now do the same calculation for cancer. For stroke. For diabetes. For liver disease. For chronic respiratory disease. For suicide. For drug overdose. For alcohol-related deaths.[6]

Add them all up—the excess deaths caused by childhood trauma across every category—and you get 1,401 deaths per day and 511,365 per year.

The bodies have always been there. We just haven't been counting them correctly.

The Hidden Epidemic

Why haven't we seen this before?

Because childhood trauma doesn't kill you all at once. It kills you slowly, over decades, through mechanisms that get labeled as something else on the death certificate.

The child who was abused doesn't die from abuse. She dies at 52 from a heart attack—and the death certificate says "myocardial infarction." But the heart attack happened because decades of elevated cortisol disrupted her cardiovascular system. Because chronic inflammation from a dysregulated nervous system caused arterial plaque buildup. Because the stress response that saved her life as a child eventually destroyed her body as an adult.

The boy who grew up with an alcoholic father doesn't die from his father's drinking. He dies at 47 from liver failure—and the death certificate says "cirrhosis." The cirrhosis happened because he became an alcoholic himself, using the same substance his father used to numb the same kind of pain. He was 5.3 times more likely to become an alcoholic because of his childhood. The bottle that killed him was first opened by his father's violence.

The teenager who was sexually molested doesn't die from molestation. She dies at 34 from a heroin overdose—and the death certificate says "opioid toxicity." But she was 11.3 times more likely to use intravenous drugs because of what happened to her. The needle that killed her was loaded by hands that touched her when she was nine years old.

This is why the epidemic stays hidden. The death certificates tell us what killed these people, but not why. They record the final mechanism but not the original wound. They count the symptoms but not the source.

And so we pour resources into treating heart disease without asking why so many hearts are failing. We fight cancer without asking why certain populations are so much more susceptible. We declare war on drugs without asking why so many people need to escape their own minds.

We keep treating symptoms while the source keeps killing.

Putting It in Perspective

Let me help you understand the scale of what we're talking about.

Childhood trauma causes 1,401 deaths per day.

That's equivalent to four fully loaded 747 airplanes crashing every single day, with no survivors. Imagine the national response if that were happening. Imagine the news coverage, the government task forces, the emergency funding, the public outcry. We would shut down the airline industry. We would declare a national emergency. We would do whatever it took to stop the carnage.

But 1,401 people dying from childhood trauma? We barely notice. Because the deaths are scattered across hospitals and homes, across death certificates that say "cancer" and "heart attack" and "overdose" instead of "childhood trauma."

Here's another comparison. At the peak of the COVID-19 pandemic, we were losing approximately 3,000 Americans per day. The nation shut down. We spent trillions of dollars. We changed how we lived, worked, and interacted. We did this because 3,000 deaths per day was intolerable.

Childhood trauma kills 1,401 Americans per day—every day, year after year, decade after decade. Not during a peak. As a permanent baseline. And we've done almost nothing about it.

Or consider this: approximately 40,000 Americans die from gun violence each year, including suicides. This has become a major political issue, with passionate advocacy on all sides. We debate it constantly. It shapes elections.

Childhood trauma kills 511,365 Americans per year. More than twelve times the gun violence total. Where is the political debate? Where is the passionate advocacy? Where are the campaigns and the legislation and the national conversation?

The silence is deafening.

The Twenty-Year Cliff

Here's the statistic that haunts me most:

People with six or more adverse childhood experiences die, on average, 20 years earlier than those with none.[7]

Twenty years.

Not a few years. Not statistically significant but practically minor. Twenty years. Two decades. The difference between meeting your grandchildren and never knowing they existed. The difference between retiring with your spouse and leaving them widowed at fifty. The difference between a full life and a life cut brutally short.

In the United States, approximately 18.6 million adults have ACE scores of 6 or higher.[8] Every one of them is standing on a 20-year cliff. Every one of them has been sentenced to early death by what happened to them before they turned 18.

That's 372 million years of life that will be lost. Not might be lost. Will be lost. Based on actuarial mathematics as reliable as any insurance company uses.[9]

In your congregation of 2,000 people, 144 of them have ACE scores of 6 or higher. Together, they represent 2,880 years of life that will be cut short. That's nearly 29 centuries of human potential—of service, of love, of wisdom passed to the next generation—gone. Because of what happened to them as children. Because no one intervened. Because no one treated the wound.

My brothers Patrick and Adam both had ACE scores of 6. They died in their forties and fifties. Right on schedule. Exactly when the actuarial tables predicted. Not from weakness or moral failure or bad choices. From childhood trauma that no one recognized and no one treated.

They didn't have to die. None of the 1,401 people dying today have to die. The research is clear that healing childhood trauma changes health outcomes.[10] That treating the wound changes the trajectory. That it is never too late to begin recovery.

But first, we have to see the wound. We have to stop counting the symptoms and start counting the source. We have to recognize that childhood trauma isn't a minor issue affecting a small population of wounded people. It is the leading cause of death in America, hiding in plain sight while we look everywhere else.

The Global Scale

Everything I've described so far has focused on the United States. But childhood trauma is not an American problem. It's a human problem.

Apply the same prevalence rates globally—and the numbers become almost incomprehensible.[11]

Of the 5.8 billion adults on Earth, approximately 4 billion have experienced at least one adverse childhood experience. Four billion wounded people walking the planet, carrying trauma encoded in their nervous systems, passing it to their children, dying early deaths that get attributed to everything except their actual cause.

Worldwide, 417 million people have ACE scores of 6 or higher. That's more than the entire population of the United States and Canada combined—all of them standing on the 20-year cliff.

The total years of life lost globally? More than 8 billion years. Eight billion years of human potential. Eight billion years of lives cut short by what happened to people when they were children.

This is not a niche issue. This is not a specialized concern for mental health professionals. This is the defining public health crisis of human civilization—and we have barely begun to recognize that it exists.

So what does this mean for the church?

It means that trauma ministry is not optional. It is not a specialized program for a small group of particularly wounded people. It is the central challenge of our time—and the church is uniquely positioned to address it.

Think about what we're dealing with. An epidemic that kills more than half a million Americans per year. An epidemic driven by wounds that occur in childhood and fester for decades before they kill. An epidemic that damages not just bodies but minds, relationships, and the very capacity to connect with God.

What institution reaches more people more regularly than the medical system? The church. What institution has the trust and access to walk with people through decades of their lives? The church. What institution has volunteers, small groups, pastoral care, and community infrastructure already in place? The church.

We already have the platform. We already have the relationships. We already have the infrastructure. What we lack is the knowledge and the training to heal trauma instead of accidentally making it worse.

Here's what should motivate us more than anything: these are our people dying. Not strangers in some distant population. Our congregants. Our families. Our children. The people we baptize and marry and bury—except we're burying them 20 years too soon because we never saw the wound that was killing them.

Every Sunday, you look out at a congregation where 70% carry childhood trauma. Where 21% are at a dramatically elevated risk for early death. Where 7%—144 people in a church of 2,000—are standing on a 20-year cliff.

Are you going to keep preaching sermons that don't see them? Keep offering ministry that doesn't reach them? Keep watching them struggle with depression, addiction, failed relationships, and chronic illness—and never connect the dots to what happened when they were children?

Or are you going to learn to see the wound? Learn to address it properly? Become one of the churches that finally closes the gap between what Jesus promised and what His people actually experience?

Today, 1,401 people will die from childhood trauma. Tomorrow, another 1,401. And the day after that. And the day after that.

The bodies keep piling up. The church keeps missing it. And the clock keeps ticking on the 20-year cliff.

In Part Two, we'll examine why the church has been blind to this crisis—not out of cruelty, but out of theological frameworks that made certain wounds invisible. First, we needed to establish what's at stake. Now you know.

What will you do about it?

Endnotes

1. Centers for Disease Control and Prevention, "Leading Causes of Death," National Center for Health Statistics, 2023, https://www.cdc.gov/nchs/fastats/leading-causes-of-death.htm.

2. Author's calculation based on ACE Study risk multipliers applied to CDC mortality data. Methodology detailed in *Bleeding in the Boardroom* (2026).

3. V. J. Felitti, R. F. Anda, D. Nordenberg, et al., "Relationship of Childhood Abuse and Household Dysfunction to Many of the Leading Causes of Death in Adults: The Adverse Childhood Experiences (ACE) Study," *American Journal of Preventive Medicine* 14, no. 4 (1998): 245–258.

4. K. Hughes, M. A. Bellis, K. A. Hardcastle, et al., "The Effect of Multiple Adverse Childhood Experiences on Health: A Systematic Review and Meta-Analysis," *The Lancet Public Health* 2, no. 8 (2017): e356–e366.

5. Felitti et al., "Relationship of Childhood Abuse," 245–258. Ischemic heart disease prevalence: 3.7% for 0 ACEs vs 5.6% for 4+ ACEs (1.5x multiplier).

6. Felitti et al., "Relationship of Childhood Abuse," 245–258. Alcoholism: 3% for 0 ACEs vs 16% for 4+ ACEs (5.3x multiplier); IV drug use: 0.3% for 0 ACEs vs 3.4% for 4+ ACEs (11.3x multiplier).

7. D. W. Brown, R. F. Anda, H. Tiemeier, et al., "Adverse Child-

hood Experiences and the Risk of Premature Mortality," *American Journal of Preventive Medicine* 37, no. 5 (2009): 389–396. Study of 17,337 adults found those with 6+ ACEs died on average 20 years earlier than those with 0 ACEs.

8. M. T. Merrick, D. C. Ford, K. A. Ports, and A. S. Guinn, "Prevalence of Adverse Childhood Experiences from the 2011–2014 Behavioral Risk Factor Surveillance System in 23 States," *JAMA Pediatrics* 172, no. 11 (2018): 1038–1044.

9. Author's calculation: 18.6 million adults with 6+ ACEs × 20 years average life lost = 372 million years.

10. K. Petruccelli, J. Davis, and T. Berman, "Adverse Childhood Experiences and Associated Health Outcomes: A Systematic Review and Meta-Analysis," *Child Abuse & Neglect* 97 (2019): 104127.

11. World Health Organization, *Global Status Report on Preventing Violence against Children* (Geneva: WHO Press, 2020). Prevalence rates applied to global adult population of 5.8 billion.

PART TWO
THE BLINDNESS

Chapter Six

The Theology That Blinds Us

> "They tie up heavy, cumbersome loads and put them on other people's shoulders, but they themselves are not willing to lift a finger to move them."
>
> –Matthew 23:4

God is not blind to it. Scripture is unambiguous about how He sees the harming of a child. The millstone passage in Matthew 18 is one of the most violent things Jesus ever said, and He said it specifically about people who damage the little ones. The church's blindness has been to the wound, not to the wrongness. That blindness is now ending—and what replaces it cannot be polite sympathy. It must be the kind of fierce, structured response Jesus modeled when He stood between the vulnerable and those who would harm them.

The church is not cruel. The church is blind.

There is a difference. Cruelty sees the wound and inflicts more pain. Blindness cannot see the wound at all, so it offers prescriptions that do not work and sometimes make things worse. The person suffering thinks, "If the pastor cannot see what is wrong with me, maybe nothing is wrong. Maybe I am just not faithful enough. Maybe I am not trying hard enough. Maybe God has given up on me."

So they try harder. Praying more. Serving more. Believing more. While the wound keeps bleeding.

The church has been blind to trauma not because it does not care, but because its theological frameworks were built before anyone knew neurobiological wounds existed. That is not an excuse. But it is an explanation. And if we are going to fix this—if we are going to finally see what we have been missing—we need to understand how we got here.

The Original Vision

Let us start with what Jesus actually did.

When Jesus stood up in the synagogue at Nazareth and announced His ministry, He did not quote a passage about doctrine or correct belief. He quoted Isaiah 61: "The Spirit of the Lord is on me, because He has anointed me to proclaim good news to the poor. He has sent me to bind up the brokenhearted, to proclaim freedom for the captives and release from darkness for the prisoners."

Bind up the brokenhearted. That was His mission statement. Not to establish an institution. Not to create theological systems. Not to protect doctrinal boundaries. To heal the wounded.

And look at what He actually did. He touched lepers when everyone else avoided them. He spoke to the Samaritan woman at the well—a woman whose five failed marriages almost certainly spoke to profound trauma and repeated victimization. He stopped a mob from stoning the woman caught in adultery and sent her away without condemnation. He cast out demons from a man so tormented he lived naked among the tombs, cutting himself with stones.

Do you see it? Jesus was trauma-responsive from day one. He did not ask what people had done wrong. He asked what had been done to them. He did not demand they clean themselves up before approaching Him. He went to them in their mess, their shame, their brokenness.

The early church understood this. They were known for caring for orphans and widows—the most traumatized people in the ancient world. They took in abandoned babies. They visited prisoners. They cared for the sick when everyone else fled. The Romans were baffled by Christians who showed up during plagues to nurse the dying, often at the cost of their own lives.

For 300 years, the church was a trauma-responsive community. That was its distinctive identity. That was why it grew.

Then something changed.

The Constantine Shift

In 313 AD, Constantine legalized Christianity. In 380 AD, Theodosius made it the official religion of the Roman Empire. And everything shifted.

Suddenly the church was not a marginalized community of wounded healers. It was an institution—with buildings to maintain, hierarchies to establish, orthodoxy to protect. The questions changed. Instead of "How do we bind up the brokenhearted?" the questions became "What do people need to believe?" and "How do we maintain order?" and "Who has authority?"

This was not malicious. It was institutional. When organizations grow, they formalize. When they formalize, they focus on systems and structures. And when the focus shifts to systems, the wounded people those systems are supposed to serve can become invisible.

The church did not stop caring about people. But it started caring more about getting people to believe the right things and do the right things than about healing the wounds that made believing and doing so difficult in the first place.

And here is what matters for our purposes: every major movement in church history since then—Catholic, Orthodox, Lutheran, Reformed, Arminian, Evangelical, Pentecostal—has inherited this institutional DNA. Each one, despite its best intentions, has reinforced a pattern that makes it nearly impossible to see trauma for what it is.

I call it the Ancient Pattern. And you already know what it is.

The Pattern That Will Not Die

Remember how I started this book? With Zara watching the moon and Kael waiting for the hunt? With the rain that stopped and the offerings that followed? With the terrible logic that when things go wrong, someone must have failed, and more sacrifice is required?

That pattern—the gods are angry and you must do something to appease them—is hardwired into human consciousness. We have been running that program for millions of years. It is in our bones. And despite what we say we believe about grace, it keeps showing up in how we practice Christianity.

Let me show you what I mean.

The Catholic Tradition

I have deep respect for my Catholic brothers and sisters. The Catholic Church has done enormous good in the world. Building hospitals, schools, and universities. Caring for the poor. Preserving learning through the Dark Ages. Producing saints whose compassion moves me to tears.

And yet.

When a traumatized person walks into a Catholic church, what do they encounter? A system of sacraments—baptism, confirmation, confession, communion, marriage, ordination, last rites—that structure the spiritual life. A clear hierarchy of authority. An emphasis on proper participation in the Mass. The message, however unintended, can sound like this: salvation involves doing certain things, in certain ways, administered by certain people with proper authority.

For someone whose nervous system is already stuck in performance mode—already convinced they are not good enough, already hypervigilant about doing things right—this framework can feel like more pressure, not less. The rituals that bring comfort to some can feel like obligations to others. The structure meant to provide stability can feel like a ladder they will never climb successfully.

I am not saying the Catholic understanding of grace is deficient. Catholic theology actually has profound resources for healing. But the lived experience for many trauma survivors in Catholic settings is one of never quite measuring up, never quite doing enough, never quite being worthy.

The ancient pattern: the gods are angry, so do more.

The Lutheran Turn

Martin Luther was himself a traumatized man. Read his biography—the harsh father, the terror-filled religious upbringing, the obsessive confession of sins real and imagined. Luther experienced what we would now recognize as severe religious anxiety, possibly driven by underlying trauma.

Luther's breakthrough was real and beautiful: justification by faith alone. Not by works. Not by earning God's favor. By trusting in Christ's completed work.

But here is the problem. Luther replaced the Catholic emphasis on rituals and sacraments with an emphasis on faith—proper belief, correct doctrine, and genuine trust. For Luther, the question was not "Have you done enough?" but "Do you believe correctly?"

For trauma survivors, this can be just as crushing. Because trauma does not just affect what we do. It affects what we can believe. A child who was abused by a trusted adult often struggles to trust anyone—including God. A child who experienced unpredictable violence often cannot believe in a world that makes sense, let alone a God who is good. A child who was told they were worthless often cannot believe they could ever be loved.

When you tell a trauma survivor that salvation depends on belief, and they discover they cannot believe—or cannot believe consistently or without terrible doubt—they conclude that something is wrong with them. Their faith is deficient. Their heart is hard. They are not really saved.

The ancient pattern, revised: the gods are angry, so believe harder.

The Calvinist Question

John Calvin took Luther's insights and systematized them. God is absolutely sovereign. Humans are totally depraved. Salvation is by grace alone—God chooses who will be saved, and those He chooses cannot fall away.

There is comfort here for some. If God chose you, you are secure. If salvation depends entirely on God's decision, you cannot screw it up.

But for trauma survivors, Calvinist theology raises a terrifying question: How do I know if I am one of the elect?

The Puritan tradition that grew from Calvinism developed elaborate tests of genuine conversion. True believers, they said, would show certain signs: grief over sin, joy in worship, growth in holiness, perseverance through trials. Ministers encouraged constant self-examination. Are you really saved? Is your faith genuine? Would a truly converted person struggle like you struggle?

For someone already prone to self-doubt, already convinced at a nervous system level that something is fundamentally wrong with them, this is poison. The questions never end. The anxiety never resolves. Every struggle becomes evidence that maybe they were never really saved in the first place.

The ancient pattern, with a twist: the gods may already be angry with you, and there is nothing you can do about it.

The Arminian Response

Arminianism arose as a counter to Calvinism. In this framework, humans have genuine free will. God offers salvation to all. People can choose to accept or reject it. And—this is the key difference—people can lose their salvation if they turn away from faith.

This sounds like freedom. And for some, it is.

But for trauma survivors, the possibility of losing salvation creates its own terror. Now every sin, every doubt, every failure becomes potentially fatal to their eternal destiny. They must maintain their faith, protect their salvation, never drift too far from the fold.

Arminian churches often emphasize recommitment. Altar calls week after week. Coming forward again to be sure. Renewing your vows to Christ. For a healthy person, these can be meaningful moments of spiritual renewal. For a trauma survivor, they can become compulsive rituals—never feeling saved enough, never confident enough, returning to the altar again and again trying to make it stick.

The ancient pattern, perpetual: the gods might become angry again, so keep sacrificing.

The Evangelical Emphasis

Modern evangelicalism blends elements of all these traditions into something distinctive. The emphasis on a personal relationship with Jesus. The importance of a conversion experience. The authority of Scripture. The call to share your faith.

At its best, evangelicalism offers something beautiful: direct, unmediated access to God. No priest required. No sacrament needed. Just you and Jesus.

But the evangelical emphasis on personal decision creates its own pressure for trauma survivors. Did you really accept Jesus? Was your conversion genuine? Have you fully surrendered? Are you really walking with the Lord?

And the evangelical culture of testimony—sharing your story of how Jesus changed your life—can be excruciating for people whose lives do not follow the expected script. "I was lost, but now I am found" works when you are actually found. But what about people who accepted Jesus at 12 and still struggle with depression at 40? What about people who have been saved for 30 years and still cannot shake the anxiety? What about people whose healing has not arrived despite decades of prayer?

The unspoken message: your faith must be inadequate. You must not have really surrendered. Something in you is blocking God's work.

The ancient pattern, internalized: the gods are angry, and it is your fault.

What Every Tradition Missed

Here is what is remarkable: every one of these traditions—Catholic, Lutheran, Calvinist, Arminian, Evangelical—has profound theological resources for healing. Each one proclaims grace. Each one insists that salvation is ultimately God's work, not ours. Each one, on paper, rejects the performance treadmill.

And yet the ancient pattern persists.

Why? Because we did not know what we did not know.

We did not know that childhood trauma rewires the brain in ways that make trust nearly impossible.

We did not know that nervous systems shaped by early adversity cannot "just believe" any more than a broken leg can "just walk."

We did not know that the guilt, shame, and self-condemnation trauma survivors feel are not a spiritual problem requiring more faith, but a neurobiological injury requiring specialized treatment.

We did not know that telling someone with a dysregulated nervous system to "rest in the Lord" is like telling someone having a panic attack to "just calm down." The intention is good. The advice is useless. The nervous system does not take orders from theology.

The church developed sophisticated frameworks for addressing spiritual problems. Sin and forgiveness. Guilt and grace. Unbelief and faith. These frameworks work beautifully for spiritual problems.

But childhood trauma is not primarily a spiritual problem. It is a neurobiological injury that produces symptoms we have misdiagnosed as spiritual problems for 2,000 years.

No wonder our prescriptions have not worked. We have been treating the wrong disease.

What Science Revealed

The Adverse Childhood Experiences Study, published in 1998, changed everything.[1] For the first time, researchers documented the massive prevalence of childhood trauma and its devastating effects across the lifespan. The neuroscience that followed showed exactly how early adversity reshapes developing brains—dysregulating stress response systems, altering brain structures, and creating biological changes that persist for decades.

Suddenly we could see what we had been missing.

That person who cannot trust God? Their amygdala learned in childhood that trust equals danger.

That person who cannot stop performing? Their nervous system is stuck in permanent threat detection, convinced that any failure will be catastrophic.

That person who keeps coming forward at altar calls? They are not spiritually deficient. They are traumatically primed to doubt their own worth, and no amount of verbal reassurance can override what their nervous system learned before they could speak.

For 2,000 years, the church has been treating these wounds as spiritual failures. We have told traumatized people they needed more faith, more prayer, more surrender, more service—when what they actually needed was trauma-responsive care.

We were not cruel. We were blind.

The science did not exist yet. The ACE Study was not published until 1998. Most of the neuroscience explaining how trauma affects the brain emerged in the 2000s and 2010s. The church could not have known what researchers had not yet discovered.

But now we know. And ignorance is no longer an excuse.

The Excruciating Irony

Here is what breaks my heart about this situation.

The church was meant to be the safest place for wounded people. Jesus came to bind up the brokenhearted. The early Christians were known for their radical care for the suffering. The whole point of the gospel is that we cannot earn our way to God—grace comes to us in our brokenness.

And yet.

For many trauma survivors, church has become one of the most painful places they can go. The place where their wounds are misdiagnosed. Where they are told their neurobiological injuries are spiritual failures. Where the ancient pattern of "do more to appease the angry gods" plays out in Christian vocabulary.

"Pray harder" means "sacrifice more."

"Trust more" means "your offering was not acceptable."

"Maybe there is unconfessed sin" means "the gods are angry because of something you did."

We say the right words about grace. But the experience for many trauma survivors is law, law, law—the relentless demand to produce what they cannot produce.

And when they cannot produce it, they leave. Or they stay but stop hoping. Or they stay and keep bleeding, quietly, invisibly, in the third row, wondering why God's peace eludes them when everyone else seems to have it figured out.

Signs of Awakening

I need to be honest about something here, because some of you reading this are already ahead of the curve—and you deserve to be seen.

Not every church is fully blind. Some have sensed that something is missing. Some have already begun to reach for what they cannot yet name.

There are churches that have partnered with licensed counselors, making therapy referrals a normal part of pastoral care rather than an admission of spiritual failure. There are congregations that have rethought their children's ministry, training volunteers to recognize trauma responses rather than punishing them as behavioral problems. There are denominations and seminaries that have started integrating trauma awareness into ministry training. Denver Seminary, for instance, recently launched a dedicated trauma-informed ministry track, recognizing that pastors need clinical knowledge alongside theological education.[2] Organizations like the North Carolina Council of Churches have developed toolkits for becoming a trauma-informed faith community.[3] Theologians like Shelly Rambo at Boston University and Serene Jones at Union Theological Seminary have begun building a scholarly framework for understanding how trauma intersects with Christian theology—work that is slowly filtering into pastoral training.[4]

These are real signs of awakening. The Spirit is already stirring.

But I want to be direct about where we are: these efforts, as courageous as they are, remain scattered, fragmented, and incomplete. A church that refers people to counselors is doing something important, but if its theology still treats trauma symptoms as spiritual failures, the referral will feel like a concession rather than a conviction. A seminary that adds a trauma course is moving in the right direction, but one elective does not transform a 2,000-year-old institutional pattern. A toolkit downloaded from a website is a start, but it is not a transformation.

What is missing is a comprehensive framework that integrates neuroscience with theology, that retrains pastoral instincts at every level—from the pulpit to the small group to the counseling office—and that equips churches not just to be trauma-informed but trauma-responsive. Knowing about trauma is one thing. Knowing what to do about it is another. And knowing how to build an entire church culture around healing rather than performance—that is the work that still lies ahead.

The churches sensing this shift are not wrong. They are early. And this book exists to give them—and every church willing to see—the comprehensive framework that scattered workshops and downloaded checklists cannot provide.

What Trauma-Responsive Theology Looks Like

So here is the question that matters: what would it look like if the church actually integrated what we now know about trauma with what we have always proclaimed about grace?

Not trauma-informed theology where we learn about trauma and add it as a footnote to our existing frameworks. Trauma-responsive theology where our understanding of the wounded brain and body actually reshapes how we read Scripture, how we preach, how we pray, and how we practice community.

The raw materials are already there. Every tradition we just surveyed contains profound resources for healing. The problem was never the theology itself. The problem was that we applied it without understanding the wound.

Here is what changes when we finally see clearly:

Justification by faith becomes liberation, not pressure. For Luther, justification meant that God accepts you apart from your works. That is a beautiful truth. But for a trauma survivor, "faith" itself can feel like another performance. Trauma-responsive theology says: God's acceptance of you does not depend on the quality of your faith or the strength of your belief. Grace reaches you before your nervous system can respond to it. You do not have to feel safe with God in order to be safe with God. The acceptance is already complete. Your nervous system will catch up—in time, with help, at whatever pace healing requires.

Sanctification becomes a healing process, not a performance review. Every tradition affirms that spiritual growth takes time. But in practice, we often treat sanctification as a report card. Are you growing fast enough? Are you holy enough? Are you producing the right fruit? Trauma-responsive theology says: sanctification includes neurobiological healing. The person who is slowly learning to trust after decades of hypervigilance is being sanctified. The person who can finally sit in silence for five minutes without their amygdala screaming is experiencing the work of the Spirit. Growth may look different for a trauma survivor than for someone with a secure attachment history—and both are real.

The body of Christ becomes a co-regulating community. Remember what we learned about co-regulation—how a calm nervous system helps a dysregulated nervous system learn to find the brake? That is what the body of Christ is supposed to be. Not a lecture hall where people receive information about God. Not a performance venue where people demonstrate their faith. A community of regulated, safe, predictable relationships where wounded nervous systems can slowly learn that the world is not as dangerous as childhood taught them. This is incarnational theology—God showing up in a body. And the body of Christ is meant to be the ongoing incarnation of that presence: safe, steady, warm, patient, real.

Confession becomes "What happened to you?" not just "What did you do?" Every tradition has some framework for confession—acknowledging what is wrong so healing can begin. Trauma-responsive theology expands confession to include what was done to us, not just what we have done. The shame a survivor carries is rarely about their own sin. It is about wounds inflicted on them that they internalized as their identity. A church that only asks "What did you do wrong?" will never reach the person whose deepest wound is what was done *to* them and no one stopped it.

Lament is given as much space as praise. The Psalms are roughly one-third lament—cries of anguish, confusion, even rage at God. But most churches devote maybe 5% of their worship to anything resembling lament. For trauma survivors, a church that only knows how to celebrate is a church that has no room for their experience. Trauma-responsive worship makes space for the cry as well as the song, for the honest "How long, O Lord?" alongside the triumphant "He is risen." This is not pessimism. It is the full range of biblical faith.

This is not a new theology. It is the original theology—the one Jesus practiced when He touched lepers and spoke to outcasts and wept at the tomb of his friend. It is what the church was before it became an institution. It is what grace has always meant, applied to wounds we can finally see.

The Blindness Does Not Have to Continue

The church is not cruel. The church has been blind.

I need to be careful here, because blindness is not the whole story and I will not pretend it is. There are churches that saw exactly what was happening and chose the institution over the child. That is not blindness. That is something else, and it has a different name, and this book is not a defense of it. What I am describing in these pages is the far more common failure—the pastor who wanted to help, tried to help, and had no idea what he was looking at. That failure deserves compassion and instruction. The other one deserves accountability. Do not let me be read as blurring the two.

But the blindness I reference here can end. You are reading this book. That means you are beginning to see. The information exists. The science is clear. The path to becoming a trauma-responsive church is documented and achievable.

The theological resources for healing have been there all along—in every tradition, in every denomination, embedded in the very doctrines that have sometimes been wielded as weapons against the wounded. Justification. Sanctification. The body of Christ. Confession. Lament. Grace upon grace.

We just could not access them because we could not see the wound.

Now we can see. And now the real work begins.

It is time to integrate what we know about neuroscience with what we proclaim about grace. It is time to become the trauma-responsive community Jesus founded 2,000 years ago.

The ancient pattern can finally be broken. The gods are not angry. The Father is weeping—weeping for His wounded children, weeping for the church that tried so hard and missed so much, weeping with the longing for His people to finally see what He has always seen.

The brokenhearted, waiting to be bound up.

Let me give you one more image for this, because I want it to stay with you.

Two Wounds. One Healer. Two Different Paths.

The framework that follows will change how you understand both the problem and the solution. Here is what I have come to believe after five years of research: There are two completely different reasons a person in your congregation might be suffering. Two different wounds, same symptoms on the surface, completely different sources—and the church has been treating only one of them.

The first wound is a theology of fear.

Performance-based religion generates cortisol. This is not a metaphor; this is biology. When a person believes they must earn God's favor—that they are never good enough, never faithful enough, always one failure away from punishment—their body responds exactly as it would to any other chronic threat. The nervous system cannot distinguish between a charging bear and an angry God. Both register as danger. Both flood the system with cortisol.

Here is the staggering good news: The Gospel of grace is a direct, measurable, biological antidote to this wound. When a person truly receives the message that they are fully accepted, fully forgiven, fully loved—not because they earned it, but as an irrevocable gift—something happens in the body. The vagus nerve activates the parasympathetic response. Cortisol drops. The amygdala quiets. Cells that were under assault begin to repair. This is what Harold Koenig's nearly 700 peer-reviewed studies have been documenting for forty years. Grace isn't just a theological concept. It is a biological intervention. Isaiah pointed toward it 700 years before Christ. Peter confirmed it.

By His wounds we are healed.

Not someday. Not metaphorically. The provision is complete and it operates at the cellular level.

The second wound is different. This is where the church has been blind.

Childhood trauma doesn't just create fearful beliefs. It physically restructures the brain. The amygdala is recalibrated to a hair trigger—not because the person lacks faith, but because the developing brain, under prolonged threat, reorganizes itself around survival. The HPA axis—the hormonal system that governs the cortisol response—gets dysregulated at a physiological level. Traumatic memories don't get filed as "past" because the hippocampus, under prolonged stress during critical developmental windows, cannot complete that process. So they live in present tense, in the body, firing cortisol as if the threat is still happening right now.

This second wound is not responding to theological information because the brain is not processing theological information normally. The trauma is jamming the signal. Grace is being broadcast at full strength, but the receiver is nonfunctional.

This is the honest answer to the question I know you are asking. Why didn't prayer heal Shannon? Why didn't forty years of genuine, sincere, faithful faith lift her depression?

It *did* work...in every channel that trauma had left open. The Gospel addressed the first wound completely. I am convinced it kept Shannon alive. The grace she received, imperfectly received, through a neurobiologically wounded system, was still enough to be the foundation that kept her from falling. Her faith was real and it was working in every room the wire could reach.

But the second wound was generating its own cortisol flood, independently, automatically, from structural damage that no theological truth could reach because the wound was blocking the channel.

There are two cortisol loads sitting in your pews. The Gospel cures one completely. The other requires that the wound be treated first—so that what the Gospel has always promised can finally be fully received.

The simplest way I know to picture this is with a single image that I want you to carry with you into everything that follows.

Grace is like electricity. The Gospel is the power source: infinite, constant, available, always flowing at full strength. The performance-based religion wound is a short circuit: the current creates pain instead of light. The Gospel of grace cuts directly through it, restores the flow, and delivers the power to every room in the house. This is what Harold Koenig's forty years of research is documenting. It heals.

The neurobiological wound is a different problem entirely. It is not a short circuit; it is a severed wire, physically cut during childhood, structurally unable to carry the current, no matter how strong the source. No amount of electricity will light a room with a severed wire. The power is not the problem. The wire is the problem.

You do not need more electricity. You need to repair the wire.

Therapy repairs the wire. Neurofeedback repairs that connection. Trauma-Responsive care repairs the wire. And when the wire is repaired, the power that was always available—full strength, never diminished, already purchased at the cross—finally flows into the rooms that have been dark for fifty years.

The electricity has always been on. The wire can now be fixed. The healing that prayer began, the church can now complete.

Endnotes

1. V. J. Felitti, R. F. Anda, D. Nordenberg, et al., "Relationship of Childhood Abuse and Household Dysfunction to Many of the Leading Causes of Death in Adults: The Adverse Childhood Experiences (ACE) Study," *American Journal of Preventive Medicine* 14, no. 4 (1998): 245–258.

2. Denver Seminary, "Equipping the Church to Heal: Denver Seminary Launches Trauma-Informed Ministry Track," *Denver Seminary News*, 2025. https://denverseminary.edu/2025/04/16/equipping-the-church-to-heal-denver-seminary-launches-trauma-informed-ministry-track/.

3. North Carolina Council of Churches, *Sacred Conversations Toolkit: Becoming a Trauma-Informed Faith Community* (Raleigh: Partners in Health and Wholeness, 2021).

4. Shelly Rambo, *Spirit and Trauma: A Theology of Remaining* (Louisville: Westminster John Knox Press, 2010); Serene Jones, *Trauma and Grace: Theology in a Ruptured World*, 2nd ed. (Louisville: Westminster John Knox Press, 2019).

Chapter Seven

The $12 Trillion Confirmation

"Even the stones will cry out."

–Luke 19:40

You might wonder what a chapter about McKinsey is doing in a book about churches.

Fair question. McKinsey is the world's most elite management consulting firm. They advise Fortune 500 companies, not congregations. They measure shareholder value, not spiritual growth. They speak the language of ROI and EBITDA, not grace and redemption.

But here is why McKinsey matters for what you are trying to understand: they just validated everything I have been telling you—without even knowing it.

In 2024 and 2025, McKinsey's Health Institute published research that documents a global workforce health crisis costing up to $12 trillion annually.[1] They surveyed 30,000 employees across 30 countries. They built comprehensive models of what is destroying worker productivity, engagement, and health.

And while they never mentioned the word "trauma," they described its effects with devastating precision.

Why does this matter for churches? Because if the world's smartest business analysts are discovering what you have been living with in your pews, then the crisis is real, it is measurable, and it is no longer something you can dismiss as "just emotional" or "just spiritual."

The secular world is waking up. The question is whether the church will wake up too—or sleep through the alarm that is ringing everywhere else.

What They Found

McKinsey's research documented findings that should sound familiar by now.

More than one in four employees globally experience symptoms of burnout—extreme tiredness, reduced ability to regulate cognitive and emotional processes, and mental distancing from their work. Workers with high burnout levels are six times more likely to leave their jobs within three to six months.[2]

Toxic behavior is the single largest predictor of burnout, accounting for more than 60% of global variance. Employees who experience unfair treatment, demeaning behavior, abusive management, or unethical conduct suffer dramatically higher rates of burnout and intent to leave.

60% of employees have experienced at least one mental health challenge at some point in their lives—anxiety, depression, distress, burnout, or substance use issues that directly impair their performance and engagement.

Only 57% of employees worldwide report good "holistic health."[3] The remaining 43%—nearly half of the global workforce—are struggling across one or more dimensions of health.

Read those numbers again. More than a quarter burned out. 60% with mental health challenges. Nearly half struggling with their overall wellbeing.

Do you think the people in your pews are somehow different from the people in workplaces? Do you imagine that trauma stops at the church door?

The same people showing up burned out to work on Monday are showing up burned out to church on Sunday. The same people experiencing anxiety in the office are experiencing anxiety in the sanctuary. The same people struggling with mental health at their jobs are struggling with mental health in your small groups.

McKinsey measured the crisis in the workforce. But the workforce goes to church. And the church is not seeing what McKinsey saw.

The Question They Never Asked

Here is what is fascinating about McKinsey's research: they documented the symptoms with extraordinary precision but never identified the root cause.

They found that toxic workplace behavior predicts burnout. But they never asked: Why does toxic behavior exist in the first place? Where does it come from?

The answer is childhood trauma. The manager who belittles subordinates is often reenacting dynamics from a childhood where they were belittled. The leader who creates fear-based cultures may be operating from a nervous system that learned early on that power equals safety. The colleague who undermines peers may be competing for resources the way they had to compete for attention as a child.

McKinsey found that 60% of employees have mental health challenges. The ACE research shows that 70% of adults carry childhood trauma. The overlap is not coincidental—it is causal. Childhood trauma is the primary driver of adult mental health conditions.

McKinsey described the bleeding. They never found the wound.

And neither has the church.

Why I Could See What McKinsey Missed

I need to tell you something about why I am the person writing this book, because it explains why I can read McKinsey's data and see what their analysts could not.

I spent decades in the world McKinsey advises. I built GenSight, a global enterprise software company serving Fortune 100 clients. I was Vice President of Worldwide Engineering at Johnson & Johnson. I hold 14 patents. I have advised organizations from NASA to the United Nations and Coca-Cola to Pfizer. I have sat in the rooms where the decisions McKinsey's reports are designed to inform actually get made.

I know that world. I speak its language. I understand its metrics.

And for most of my career, I was just as blind as McKinsey is now. I could see the dysfunction—the toxic leadership, the burnout, the disengagement, the revolving door of talented people who kept leaving—but I could not see the cause. I measured what was measurable and missed what was invisible.

Then I started writing a memoir about my family—14 children growing up in Kankakee, Illinois. And as I wrote, I began to understand what happened to us. The chaos. The dysfunction. The trauma that shaped every one of us in ways we never understood. The brothers I lost to heroin. The patterns that repeated across generations.

That is when I found the ACE research. And everything I had seen in decades of corporate life suddenly made sense. The toxic manager was not a bad person—he was a wounded person running survival programs written in childhood. The disengaged employee was not lazy—she was dissociated, her nervous system in permanent freeze. The brilliant executive who self-destructed was not weak—his pain was greater than his coping capacity.

I could see what McKinsey missed because I had lived on both sides. I had been the corporate executive measuring symptoms I could not explain. And I had been the trauma survivor who did not know he was one.

That intersection—between the boardroom and the wound—is where this book lives. And it is where the church needs to stand if it wants to meet this moment.

Why This Matters for Your Ministry

When the world's most credible analysts spend millions of dollars researching workplace health and arrive at conclusions that point directly to childhood trauma—even if they do not name it—you are witnessing a moment of convergence.

The secular world is discovering what the church should have known all along: that people are wounded, that those wounds affect everything, and that organizations not equipped to address those wounds will pay an enormous price.

McKinsey framed it in economic terms: $12 trillion in lost productivity and healthcare costs. But the church does not measure success in dollars. You measure it in lives transformed, families healed, communities restored.

By that measure, the cost of ignoring trauma is even higher.

Every person who leaves your church because they could not find healing—cost. Every volunteer who burns out because their nervous system could not sustain the demands—cost. Every pastor who quits ministry because the weight became unbearable—cost. Every suicide among your congregation that might have been prevented—cost beyond calculation.

McKinsey helped CEOs see that workforce health is not a "soft" issue—it is the hardest of hard business realities. The same logic applies to ministry. Trauma in your pews is not a pastoral footnote. It is the central challenge you face.

The Spiritual Dimension McKinsey Found

Here is something McKinsey discovered that should make church leaders sit up straight.

In October 2024, McKinsey Health Institute released findings on "spiritual health" in the workplace.[4] They drew on a global survey of 41,000 people across 26 countries and found something remarkable: spiritual health was one of the strongest predictors of employee productivity and wellbeing.

Let me be clear about what they mean by "spiritual health." They are not talking about religious practice specifically. They are talking about meaning, purpose, and connection to something larger than oneself—what researchers call a "transcendent" dimension of human experience.

Their findings:

Employees with low holistic health who reported high spiritual health functioned better than colleagues with good holistic health but low spiritual health. Meaning and purpose were protective even when everything else was struggling.

Spiritual health was directly correlated with intent to stay at a job, even more than other dimensions of wellbeing. People who find meaning in their work stay longer than people who are merely satisfied.

The McKinsey researchers were blunt about it: spiritual health is real, and any serious attempt at holistic health that leaves it out is incomplete.

This is McKinsey—the same firm that advises the most hard-nosed corporations in the world—telling business leaders that the spiritual dimension matters. That you cannot maximize human flourishing without addressing meaning, purpose, and transcendence.

Where does meaning come from? Where is purpose found? Where do people connect to transcendence?

For billions of people, the answer is church.

The church should be uniquely positioned to offer what McKinsey found people desperately need. We have two thousand years of wisdom about meaning, purpose, and connection to the divine. We have communities built around transcendence. We have Scripture, prayer, worship, fellowship—all the raw materials for spiritual health.

But we can only deliver on that potential if we first address the trauma that blocks people's capacity to receive it.

You cannot experience meaning when your nervous system is stuck in survival mode. You cannot find purpose when you are drowning in shame from childhood. You cannot connect to transcendence when you cannot trust anyone—including God.

McKinsey found the destination. The church has the destination. But trauma blocks the path.

The Wellness Programs That Fail

McKinsey also documented something the corporate world desperately needs to hear: most wellness programs do not work.[5]

Despite billions invested in yoga classes, meditation apps, gym memberships, and stress management workshops, the needle has not moved on employee wellbeing. Some programs show marginal benefits. Many show none. A few may actually make things worse.

McKinsey's explanation: "Many workplace wellness programs underperform not because they are flawed, but because they do not align with the way people actually work and live."[6]

But the deeper reason is one McKinsey did not name: wellness programs designed for healthy adults do not work for traumatized adults. And traumatized adults constitute 70% of the population.

You cannot yoga your way out of a dysregulated nervous system. You cannot meditate past a brain wired for threat detection. You cannot breathe through decades of accumulated biological damage from childhood adversity.

This is why church programs often fail, too.

Bible studies do not heal trauma. Prayer groups do not rewire nervous systems. Sermons on peace do not create peace in bodies that never experienced safety. Small groups cannot provide what they are not designed to provide.

These programs—like corporate wellness programs—are designed for people with intact stress response systems. For people who can "take in" what is being offered because their nervous systems allow receptivity. For people who can "just believe" because their brains were not shaped by early experiences that made belief feel dangerous.

For the 70% carrying trauma, we need something more. Something designed for wounded people. Something trauma-responsive.

McKinsey discovered that you cannot wellness-program your way to health when the underlying wound remains untreated. Churches need to learn the same lesson—and learn it faster than corporate America is learning it.

The Convergence

Here is what I want you to see.

The world's most sophisticated researchers are documenting a crisis that the church has been living with for 2,000 years. They are measuring symptoms the church has been treating—unsuccessfully—with spiritual prescriptions alone. They are validating with data what you may have felt in your gut: something is deeply wrong, and our current approaches are not working.

But they are also discovering something the church should claim as its birthright: that meaning matters. That purpose heals. That transcendence is essential to human flourishing.

This is your moment.

The secular world is waking up to trauma. They are beginning to see what they missed. They are searching for solutions—solutions that, at their deepest level, point toward the very things the church exists to provide.

But the church will not be positioned to meet this moment if it remains blind to the wound. You cannot lead people to the meaning they need if you first cause more damage by misdiagnosing their pain. You cannot offer the purpose they are desperate for if you tell them their neurobiological injuries are spiritual failures.

McKinsey is sounding an alarm. The corporate world is scrambling to respond. The church has an opportunity to step forward with something the business consultants cannot provide. Not just interventions and programs, but genuine healing. Not just productivity improvement, but transformation. Not just wellness, but wholeness. Not just health, but thriving.

Will we take it?

I need to answer the deeper question first, because some of you are holding a specific verse, and it deserves a direct response.

"Ask and you shall receive."

–Matthew 7:7

Shannon asked. For 50 years, she asked. Jamie asked for 30. I asked for decades.

And the healing we prayed for didn't come. Does that mean the promise is false?

No. It means we have been misunderstanding what we received.

Shannon asked for total healing. She received total healing—in the form that prayer was designed to deliver. She received a foundation that held her when she had every biological reason to fall through it. She received enough grace to stay out of the addiction spiral that claimed others with her exact wound profile. She received connection to God through a nervous system that was structurally impaired in its ability to receive that connection fully. She survived a body that the ACE research says should have begun its fatal disintegration decades earlier. That is not a failed prayer. That is an answered prayer. A promise kept.

What she didn't yet receive was the neurobiological repair. Not because God withheld it, but because she was using only one of the two tools He placed in the world for complete healing.

Think of it this way: For most of human history, people prayed faithfully for healing from cancer and rarely received it. Did prayer fail them? No. Prayer delivered everything prayer was designed to deliver—peace, endurance, the presence of God in the suffering, sometimes miraculous exceptions—but the full biological provision for cancer treatment required the development of oncology, surgery, radiation, chemotherapy. We do not say prayer failed the cancer patients of the fifteenth century because chemotherapy hadn't been invented yet. We say God provided everything prayer could provide, and He also placed in the world—in His time—the tools to address the biological wound. Now that we have both, the provision is more complete than it has ever been.

Childhood trauma is the cancer of this generation. Prayer has been providing everything prayer can provide—and that provision has kept millions alive who should have died. The neurobiological repair tools—EMDR, neurofeedback, somatic therapy, trauma-focused care—are the oncology that God placed in this specific generation, in this specific century, to complete what prayer began. We are not choosing between them. We are, for the first time, able to use both.

"Ask and you shall receive" is more gloriously, completely true than it has ever been, because the full delivery mechanism is finally available.

Endnotes

1. McKinsey Health Institute, *Thriving Workplaces: How Employers Can Improve Productivity and Change Lives*, McKinsey & Company, January 16, 2025, https://www.mckinsey.com/mhi/our-insights/thriving-workplaces-how-employers-can-improve-productivity-and-change-lives.

2. McKinsey Health Institute, "Addressing Employee Burnout: Are You Solving the Right Problem?" McKinsey Health Institute, May 27, 2022, https://www.mckinsey.com/mhi/our-insights/addressing-employee-burnout-are-you-solving-the-right-problem.

3. McKinsey Health Institute, *Reframing Employee Health: Moving Beyond Burnout to Holistic Health*, McKinsey & Company, November 2, 2023, https://www.mckinsey.com/mhi/our-insights/reframing-employee-health-moving-beyond-burnout-to-holistic-health.

4. McKinsey Health Institute, "Beyond 9 to 5: The Power of Spiritual Health in the Workplace," *McKinsey Future of Asia Podcast*, McKinsey & Company, October 4, 2024, https://www.mckinsey.com/featured-insights/future-of-asia/future-of-asia-podcasts/beyond-9-to-5-the-power-of-spiritual-health-in-the-workplace.

5. McKinsey Health Institute, *From Potential to Practical: Fueling Performance with Proven Workplace Health Interventions*, McKin-

sey & Company, January 7, 2026, https://www.mckinsey.com/mhi/our-insights/from-potential-to-practical-fueling-performance-with-proven-workplace-health-interventions.

6. McKinsey Health Institute, *From Potential to Practical.*

Chapter Eight

The Shepherds Are Bleeding, Too

"Secure your own oxygen mask before assisting others."
–Universal Airline Safety Announcement

Before we talk about the sheep, we need to talk about the shepherds.

Because here is something almost no one in church leadership wants to acknowledge: pastors and church leaders carry more of a particular kind of childhood wounding than the people sitting in front of them.

Not more trauma overall. More of the relational kind—the kind that teaches a child to read a room, absorb a mood, and hold a family together before they are old enough to know they are doing it.

The Numbers No One Wants to See

Researchers at Duke University studied 535 seminarians at a mainline Protestant seminary and compared them against a demographically matched national sample. The seminarians reported higher rates of emotional abuse, of childhood sexual abuse, and of growing up with someone who had a mental illness.[1] A separate study of Black clergy and religious leaders found the same shape in different form, significantly higher rates of emotional neglect, parental separation or divorce, mental illness in the household, and an incarcerated family member.[2]

Read those findings carefully, because they are more interesting than a headline number. Total childhood adversity scores were not dramatically higher. What was higher was a particular kind of adversity—the relational kind. Emotional neglect. A parent who was not available. A household holding something it could not name. The precise childhood that produces an adult who is extraordinarily good at sensing what other people need. A 2021 Barna Group study reported devastating findings.[3]

- 38% of pastors have seriously considered quitting full-time ministry in the past year.

- 46% report struggling with depression at levels requiring professional intervention.

- 70% feel grossly underpaid for their responsibilities.

- 42% report being often or always overwhelmed by their duties.

And in a finding that should alarm everyone: 29% of pastors reported feeling "emotionally exhausted" most or all of the time. Not occasionally tired. Chronically depleted.

These are not pastors complaining about busy seasons. These are shepherds who are bleeding while trying to tend their flocks.

Why Would Wounded People Become Pastors?

It might seem counterintuitive that people with high trauma histories would be drawn to ministry. But if you understand trauma, it makes perfect sense.

People who experienced childhood chaos often develop extraordinary sensitivity to others' emotions—a survival skill called hypervigilance. In a dangerous home, reading the room accurately could mean the difference between safety and violence. That same ability to sense what others are feeling makes someone seem unusually compassionate, unusually attentive, unusually gifted at caring for people.

People who grew up feeling helpless often seek positions where they can help others. If they could not save themselves as a child, perhaps they can save others as an adult. Ministry offers that opportunity.

People who experienced profound pain often search for meaning in that pain. Religion offers a framework for understanding suffering—for redeeming what felt irredeemable. Ministry becomes a way to transform personal wounds into purpose.

People who were shamed in childhood often seek approval through performance. Ministry provides constant opportunities to perform—sermons, counseling, leadership—and constant feedback on whether you are doing it well.

People who felt unloved sometimes become relentless in loving others. If no one cared for them, they will care for everyone. The emptiness becomes fuel for a lifetime of service.

These are not character flaws. They are adaptations. Many of them produce genuine gifts for ministry. But when the underlying trauma remains unaddressed, those same adaptations become vulnerabilities.

The **hypervigilant pastor** who senses everything eventually exhausts their nervous system from constant scanning.

The **helper** who could not save themselves eventually burns out from trying to save everyone else.

The **meaning-maker** who never processed their own suffering eventually collapses under the weight of others' pain.

The **performer** who seeks approval never rests, never feels adequate, never knows when enough is enough.

The **person who loves relentlessly** to fill their own emptiness never stops to receive love—and the emptiness remains.

This is why pastors burn out at alarming rates. This is why ministry marriages fail. This is why some pastors end their own lives.

Pastor David

David planted his church at 28 with a fire in his gut and an ache he could not name.

He was good at this. Everyone said so. The church grew from 40 people in a rented school cafeteria to 600 in a permanent building within five years. David preached with conviction, counseled with empathy, and seemed to have an almost supernatural ability to sense when someone in the congregation was hurting. People said he had the gift of discernment. What David had was hypervigilance—a nervous system trained by a volatile, alcoholic father to read every room for danger.

For 15 years, David ran at full speed. He answered every call, attended every hospital visit, mediated every conflict, preached every Sunday. He could not say no—not because he did not want to, but because some part of him believed that if he stopped being useful, he would stop being loved. That belief was not theological. It was neurological. It was written into his wiring by a childhood where love was conditional and withdrawal of approval meant danger.

His wife, Sarah, saw it first. She told him he was disappearing—that the man she married was being consumed by the ministry he built. David heard her concern and felt it as criticism. His amygdala translated "I'm worried about you" into "You're not enough." He worked harder.

By year 12, David was drinking a bottle of wine most nights to quiet the noise in his head. By year 14, he was having panic attacks in his office before services—full-body shaking, chest tightness, the certainty that something terrible was about to happen. He would compose himself, walk to the pulpit, and preach about God's peace with a nervous system that was screaming.

The breaking point came on an ordinary Tuesday. David was sitting in his car in the church parking lot and realized he could not make himself go inside. Not because anything bad was waiting for him. Because his body was done. His nervous system had finally hit the wall that 15 years of performance had been racing toward.

David's associate pastor found him there 45 minutes later, still sitting, engine off, staring straight ahead.

What followed was the hardest and most important year of David's life. With Sarah's insistence and his associate pastor's support, David took a three-month sabbatical. He found a Christian therapist who specialized in trauma and began the work he had been avoiding since he was eight years old—the work of understanding what his father's rage and unpredictability had done to his developing brain, his attachment system, and his capacity for rest.

The therapy was brutal. David had to sit with feelings he had been outrunning for decades. He had to grieve the childhood he did not have. He had to admit that his extraordinary ministry gifts—the empathy, the drive, the ability to read any room—were not just spiritual gifts. They were survival skills forged in a dangerous home, and they had been running him into the ground.

But David also discovered something remarkable. As his nervous system began to regulate—as he learned to find the brake pedal he had never known existed—his ministry transformed. He came back from sabbatical and people noticed immediately. Not because he announced his diagnosis. Because he was different. Calmer. More present. Less frantic. He preached with the same conviction but without the desperate energy. He counseled without absorbing everyone else's pain. He could sit with someone in crisis without his own nervous system going into overdrive.

For the first time in his ministry, David was leading from wholeness rather than from wound.

His church did not collapse during his absence. It grew. The leaders David had been too anxious to trust stepped up. The congregation learned that their pastor was human, and the sky did not fall. And David learned something he now tells every pastor who will listen: "You cannot give what you do not have. I was trying to give people peace from a body that had never known it. Once I found it for myself, I could finally offer it for real."

The Vicious Cycle

David's story is not unusual. It is the norm.

Traumatized pastors leading traumatized congregations create a devastating cycle.

- The pastor who cannot set boundaries because childhood taught them their needs do not matter will work themselves into the ground while their congregation demands more.

- The pastor who needs approval will avoid difficult conversations, allowing problems to fester until they explode.
- The pastor who feels like an imposter will compensate by performing relentlessly, projecting confidence they do not feel, and feeling increasingly fraudulent as the gap between image and reality grows.
- The pastor who was taught to suppress emotions will struggle to create space for others' emotions and may inadvertently shame congregants who express theirs.
- The pastor who was shamed for weakness will project strength while crumbling inside—modeling for the congregation that struggling is not acceptable.

And the congregation, taking cues from their leader, will hide their own wounds, perform their own faith, and suffer in the same silence they see modeled from the pulpit.

Wounded shepherds produce wounded flocks who expect to be tended by wounded shepherds who produce wounded flocks who. . .

The cycle continues until something breaks.

What Breaking Looks Like

Sometimes what breaks is the pastor's health. The body keeps score. Decades of suppressed trauma, chronic stress, and unrelenting demands produce heart attacks, strokes, autoimmune disorders, and early death.

Sometimes what breaks is the pastor's family. Ministry-related divorces are heartbreakingly common. Pastors' kids who abandon faith as adults. Spouses who feel like widows to a congregation they resent.

Sometimes what breaks is the pastor's ministry. Moral failures that seem to come out of nowhere—but never actually come from nowhere. They come from wounds that festered untended, coping mechanisms that turned toxic, isolation that became unbearable.

And sometimes what breaks is the pastor's will to live.

Clergy suicide rates are difficult to measure accurately because many are unreported or misclassified. But the anecdotal evidence is devastating. Every month seems to bring news of another pastor who took their own life. Social media fills with tributes and shock: *He seemed so strong. She helped so many people. We never knew they were struggling.*

Of course they seemed strong. That is what trauma survivors do. They mask. They perform. They care for everyone except themselves.

Until they cannot anymore.

Why Pastors Do Not Get Help

If the crisis is this severe, why aren't more pastors seeking treatment? Because the barriers to help are stacked against them in ways that most congregants never see.

The money is not there. The average pastor's salary in America hovers around $50,000 to $55,000, and many earn significantly less—especially in smaller churches that lack the budget for competitive compensation. Quality trauma therapy typically costs $150 to $250 per session, often weekly, for months or even years. Most pastoral compensation packages do not include mental health benefits, and many church insurance plans have limited behavioral health coverage. For a pastor supporting a family on a modest income, consistent therapy is not just inconvenient—it is financially impossible. The people most likely to need trauma treatment are often the least able to afford it.

The fishbowl will not let them. Pastors, especially in small to mid-sized congregations, live in a fishbowl. Their car is recognized. Their schedule is scrutinized. In a small town, being seen walking into a therapist's office is not a private act—it is a potential congregational crisis. Word travels. Elders worry. Search committees for the next pastoral hire quietly add "stable mental health" to their unwritten criteria. The lack of confidentiality in close-knit church communities creates a surveillance dynamic that makes seeking help feel professionally dangerous.

The theology works against them. Many pastors were trained in traditions that view therapy with suspicion. Counseling is "worldly." Psychology is "secular humanism." If the Bible is sufficient for all matters of life and faith, then needing a therapist implies that Scripture is not enough—which feels like a betrayal of the very foundation they have built their lives on. A pastor who seeks trauma therapy may face not just personal doubt but genuine theological conflict: *Am I admitting that God is not sufficient? Am I turning to the world for what only God can provide?* These questions are not trivial. For someone whose identity is built on faith, pursuing clinical treatment can feel like apostasy.

The role will not allow it. The unspoken expectation in most churches is that the pastor is the one who has it together. Congregants bring their problems to the pastor. The pastor does not bring problems to congregants. This creates an impossible dynamic: the person most exposed to the congregation's collective pain is the one least permitted to acknowledge their own. Admitting trauma, seeking therapy, or—God forbid—requesting a leave of absence to heal can be interpreted by boards and congregations as evidence of unfitness for the role. Pastors have been fired for less. The fear is not paranoid. It is based on what they have watched happen to colleagues.

The isolation is total. Most pastors do not have peers they trust enough to be vulnerable with. Other pastors are potential competitors, gossips, or judges. Denominational leaders are evaluators, not confidants. The congregation is the flock they tend, not the community that tends them. And spouses, even the most supportive ones, carry their own burdens and cannot be their pastor's therapist. The result is a kind of professional solitary confinement—surrounded by people but known by no one. And isolation is not just lonely. For a trauma survivor, isolation removes the very thing healing requires: safe and honest human connection.

These barriers are not excuses. They are real, structural obstacles that the church has created—often without realizing it—that prevent its own leaders from getting well. And until the church addresses these barriers systemically, it will continue to lose pastors to burnout, breakdown, moral failure, and death.

The Mirror Before the Window

In the companion book to this one—*Bleeding in the Boardroom*—I introduce a concept called the Mirror and the Window. Before you can truly help others with their trauma, you must first examine your own. The Mirror before the Window.

This is not optional for church leaders. It is essential.

You cannot lead a congregation to healing places you have never visited yourself. You cannot create safety for others if you have never experienced safety. You cannot teach rest if you do not know how to rest. You cannot model surrender if you are white-knuckling your way through ministry.

And you cannot see the trauma in your congregation if you have not looked at the trauma in yourself.

This is not about disqualifying wounded people from ministry. If we did that, we would have no ministers. The 70% prevalence means most pastors have experienced childhood adversity. The question is not whether leaders have trauma. The question is whether they have done the work to heal—or whether they are bleeding on the people they are supposed to serve.

What Healing Looks Like *Practically*

Let me be clear about what I am asking of church leaders. And let me be practical, because platitudes about "self-care" do not pay for therapy or convince elder boards.

First, look in the Mirror. Take the ACE questionnaire. Be honest with yourself about what you experienced in childhood. Consider whether patterns in your ministry—workaholism, conflict avoidance, need for approval, difficulty delegating, chronic exhaustion—might trace back to early experiences. This costs nothing and takes 10 minutes. But it may change everything about how you understand yourself.

Second, find a trauma-responsive therapist. Not just any counselor. Someone trained in evidence-based trauma treatment: EMDR, Somatic Experiencing, or other modalities designed to address neurobiological injury, not just talk about feelings. Look for someone who understands both trauma and ministry. Organizations like the American Association of Christian Counselors maintain directories. Ask specifically: "Are you trained in trauma-focused therapy?" If the answer is vague, keep looking.

Third, solve the money problem. This is where the church needs to step up. Boards and denominations should budget for pastoral mental health the way they budget for continuing education, because that is exactly what it is. If your church cannot afford it, explore sliding-scale therapists, nonprofit counseling centers, or denominational benevolence funds. Some organizations offer reduced-rate therapy specifically for clergy. If you are a board member reading this: adding a mental health line item to your pastor's compensation package may be the most important investment you make this year. It is cheaper than a pastoral search when your current pastor collapses.

Fourth, create protected space. Pastors need confidential, accountable relationships outside their congregations. Peer groups of pastors who meet with a trained facilitator. A spiritual director who is not part of the church hierarchy. A therapist who has no connection to the congregation. The goal is at least one relationship where the pastor can be fully honest without professional consequences. If you are a denominational leader, build these structures. Fund them. Make them normal. Your pastors are dying for lack of them.

Fifth, plan for the possibility of a sabbatical. Some pastors will discover that their healing requires more than weekly therapy sessions. They may need extended time—a month, a season, even a year. This terrifies most pastors because they assume the church cannot survive without them and that requesting time off is career suicide. Both assumptions are usually wrong. Churches that have navigated pastoral sabbaticals well report stronger lay leadership, deeper congregational ownership, and pastors who return transformed. If you are a pastor, talk to your board before you are in crisis. Frame it as an investment, not an emergency. If you are a board member, make sabbatical policy proactive, not reactive. The pastor who takes a healing sabbatical at the right time is the pastor who stays for 20 more years. The one who never stops is the one you lose.

Sixth, model the journey. You do not have to share your diagnosis. You do not have to stand at the pulpit and narrate your therapy sessions. But you can say: "I am working on my own health." You can normalize therapy the way you normalize going to the doctor. You can create a culture where admitting struggle is strength, not weakness. The congregation takes its cues from you. If you pretend everything is fine while you are dying inside, they will pretend too. If you acknowledge that leaders need healing too, you give them permission to seek their own.

The Cost of Ignorance

If shepherds do not heal, flocks do not heal.

If pastors continue burning out at current rates, the church will face a leadership crisis on top of its membership crisis. Who will lead the congregations when the current generation of pastors collapses?

If ministry families keep disintegrating, the human cost will be incalculable. How many more pastors' kids will abandon faith? How many more ministry marriages will end?

If pastoral suicides continue, we will lose not just individual leaders but the moral authority to speak about hope at all. How can we proclaim resurrection when our own are choosing death?

This is not someone else's problem. If you are a church leader reading this, it is your problem. And if you are in a congregation led by an overwhelmed, traumatized, unhealed pastor, it is affecting you whether you know it or not.

The Hope: Healing is Possible

Remember Jamie from Chapter 3? Thirty years of depression, unresponsive to prayer alone. Seven sessions of EMDR therapy, and the cloud lifted. He was healed not by abandoning faith but by adding competent trauma treatment to his faith.

Remember Pastor David? Fifteen years of running on fumes, a nervous system that finally hit the wall. Three months of sabbatical, a year of trauma therapy, and he came back transformed—not performing ministry but inhabiting it. His congregation did not just survive his absence. They grew.

Pastors can heal, too. Neuroplasticity means the brain can change at any age. Trauma that has been carried for decades can be resolved. Nervous systems that have been dysregulated for years can learn to regulate. The body keeps score, but the score can change.

I have seen pastors who did the work. Who looked in the mirror. Who got help. Who emerged from treatment with a depth and authenticity they never had before. Their preaching changed. Their counseling changed. Their presence changed. They stopped performing ministry and started inhabiting it.

Their congregations noticed. Not because the pastor announced their diagnosis. Because wounded people recognize genuine healing. They know the difference between someone who talks about grace and someone who has experienced it at a cellular level.

These healed shepherds become the most effective trauma-responsive leaders. They see what others miss because they have been there. They create safety because they know what safety feels like. They do not shame struggle because they have struggled. They do not offer platitudes because they know platitudes do not help.

This is what becomes possible when shepherds heal. And this is why the transformation of the church must begin with the transformation of its leaders.

Secure your own oxygen mask before assisting others.

Look in the Mirror before you look through the Window.

Heal so that you can lead others to healing.

The sheep need shepherds who are not bleeding. They deserve shepherds who have done their own work. And the good news is that healing is available—if leaders have the courage to pursue it.

Endnotes

1. Anna Holleman, Laura Upenieks, and David Eagle, "Adverse Childhood Experiences Among Seminarians: Personal Experiences of Trauma and Implications for Pastoral Well-Being and Ministerial Training," *Journal of Psychology and Theology* 52, no. 1 (2024): 3–17, https://doi.org/10.1177/00916471231206361.

2. Eric M. Brown, Eu Gene Chin, David C. Wang, Blaire A. Lewis, Christin Fort, Laura E. Captari, Sarah A. Crabtree, and Steven J. Sandage, "Adverse Childhood Experiences, Religious Coping, and Congregational Support among Black Clergy and Religious Leaders," *Religions* 15, no. 4 (2024): 396, .

3. Barna Group, "38% of U.S. Pastors Have Thought About Quitting Full-Time Ministry in the Past Year," Barna Group, November 16, 2021, https://www.barna.com/research/pastors-well-being/.

PART THREE

THE HEMORRHAGE

Chapter Nine

The Great Exodus

> "They are not leaving because they stopped believing. They are leaving because they could not keep bleeding."
>
> –Michael Menard

THE AMERICAN CHURCH IS dying.

That statement might sound alarmist. It is not. It is simply what the data shows.

In 1972, 90% of Americans identified as Christian.[1] By 2020, that number had dropped to 64%. The slide continues. Church membership has fallen from 70% in 1999 to under 50% today—the first time in American history that fewer than half of adults belong to a church, synagogue, or mosque.[2] The "nones"—people claiming no religious affiliation—have doubled in 20 years. Among young adults, nearly 40% claim no religious identity.[3]

We are not talking about a small correction. We are talking about a generational collapse.

Here is the connection we have been building toward: if up to 70% of your flock is bleeding from childhood trauma, then the church is not just wounded. The church is hemorrhaging.

But here is what the statistics do not tell you: who is leaving and why.

They Came Looking for Healing

Church leaders offer various explanations for the exodus—and many of them contain real truth. Some people leave over intellectual questions about theology. Some leave because of moral objections to church positions on social issues. Some leave disillusioned by church politics, leadership scandals, or financial misconduct. Some leave because the way Americans relate to institutions has fundamentally shifted—younger generations are less likely to commit to any organized body, religious or otherwise.

These are all real factors. I am not dismissing them, and this book is not pretending to address all the reasons people walk away from church.

But underneath the reasons that get the most attention, there is one that almost nobody is talking about, and it may be the most significant of them all.

Many people—far more than we have acknowledged—go to church because they are hurting. They may not use that language. They may not even know that is why they are there. But something in them is broken, and something in them hopes that God's people can help fix it.

They come wounded, looking for healing.

And what do they find?

"Pray harder."

"Trust more."

"Maybe there is unconfessed sin."

"You just need more faith."

They come bleeding, and the church hands them a Band-Aid and a guilt trip.

This chapter is about that group. The ones who did not leave over doctrine or politics or scandal. The ones who left because the church could not see their wounds—or worse, saw them and called them sin.

Sarah

Let me tell you what the exodus actually looks like.

Sarah grew up in the church. Third-generation member of her congregation. She loved Jesus, loved worship, loved belonging to something bigger than herself.

But Sarah also struggled with depression that started when she was a teenager—depression she later connected to emotional neglect in her childhood. For years, she tried to "pray through" it. When that did not work, she went to her pastor, who told her that depression was a spiritual battle she needed to fight with faith.

When she finally saw a therapist—feeling like she was betraying her church by doing so—the healing began. But she felt like she had to hide it.

One Sunday, the pastor preached about how medication was "a crutch for people who do not trust God." Sarah had just started antidepressants that were finally helping. She felt like she had been punched in the stomach.

She stopped going that day.

It has been five years. She still believes in God. She does not believe in church.

Daniel

Daniel came to faith in his thirties after a friend invited him to a small group. He loved the Bible teaching and the community. But Daniel had grown up in an abusive home, and he carried scars he did not know how to name.

When the church did a series on forgiveness, the pastor emphasized that Christians must forgive everyone, immediately and completely. Daniel tried. He could not. The rage toward his father would not go away no matter how many times he prayed.

When he confessed his struggle, an elder told him his unforgiveness was sin, and that bitterness was blocking God's blessing in his life.

Daniel concluded that he must be too faulty to be a real Christian. He left.

What Daniel did not know—what the elder did not know—is that trauma rewires the brain's capacity for forgiveness. You cannot "just forgive" when your amygdala is screaming danger. Forgiveness for trauma survivors is a process that often requires therapeutic support, not a one-time decision.

Michelle

Michelle was a pastor's wife. She was also a survivor of childhood sexual abuse—something she had never told anyone, including her husband.

For years, she performed the role perfectly. Smiling at everyone, leading the women's ministry, hosting the parties. Dying inside.

When she finally broke down and told a trusted friend at church what had happened to her as a child, the friend meant well but said the wrong thing: "Have you forgiven him? Because unforgiveness is the root of a lot of problems."

Michelle realized the church had no framework for understanding what happened to her except as something requiring her forgiveness. Her wound became her sin. Her victimization became her failure.

She and her husband left ministry. He pastors a small church now in another state. She goes to therapy and works from home. She is not sure she will ever go back to church.

The Pattern

Sarah, Daniel, and Michelle—they are not unusual. They are the pattern.

Across America, people who came to church carrying wounds left because the church could not see them. Or worse—saw them and blamed them.

Now, let me be fair. As I said at the start of this chapter, the exodus has many causes. Cultural shifts are real. Generational changes are real. Intellectual doubts, institutional distrust, political disillusionment—all of these contribute, and this book does not pretend otherwise.

But we can be certain that unaddressed trauma is a factor. A significant one. Possibly the most significant of all, because it operates beneath the surface of the other reasons. The person who leaves over "theological questions" may actually be leaving because the theology they were handed made their suffering worse. The person who leaves over "church politics" may actually be leaving because the political dynamics in the congregation triggered their childhood experience of chaotic, unsafe authority. The person who says they just "drifted away" may have been slowly drowning and no one noticed.

When 70% of your congregation carries trauma and your only prescription is "pray harder," you are going to lose people. Not all of them—but enough to matter. Enough to turn a healthy church into a declining one. Enough to turn a declining church into an empty building.

They were told their neurobiological injuries were spiritual failures. Their trauma responses were labeled sin. Their inability to "just believe" or "just forgive" or "just trust" was taken as evidence of inadequate faith.

And eventually, they got tired. Tired of trying to heal with tools that do not work for trauma. Tired of being told their struggles proved something wrong with their relationship with God. Tired of bleeding in the pews while everyone around them seemed to have it figured out.

So they left.

Not because they stopped believing in God. Many of them still believe. Not because they do not want community. Many of them ache for it. Not because they are hostile to religion. Many of them mourn what they lost.

They left because they could not keep bleeding in a place that could not see the blood.

And if you are one of those people—if you left because the church could not hold your pain, could not see your wounds, could not help you heal—I want you to hear something that maybe no one in the church ever told you: You are not broken. You did not fail God. You survived. And the fact that you left a place that was hurting you may have been the healthiest decision you ever made.

Two Kinds of Leaving

It is important to distinguish between two groups among those who left because of unaddressed trauma.

Some left the church and left faith entirely. They concluded that if this is what Christianity produces—judgment, shame, ineffective help—then maybe Christianity is not true after all. They became atheists, agnostics, or "spiritual but not religious."

Others left the church but kept their faith. They still pray. They still read Scripture. They still love Jesus. They just cannot do church anymore—not after what they experienced. They became the "dechurched faithful"—believers without belonging.

Both groups represent losses. But they are different losses.

The people who lost faith may have lost it because the church gave them a false choice: either accept our approach to your wounds, or reject God entirely. When the church's approach did not work, they concluded the whole thing was false.

The people who kept faith but left church may be the most tragic losses of all. They still believe. They still want to belong. But they have concluded that the church—at least as they have experienced it—is not safe for wounded people.

Both groups could be reclaimed. But only by a church that learns to see trauma and respond to it properly.

What We Are Losing

The exodus is not just about numbers. It is about who we are losing.

We are losing the wounded healers—people whose trauma gave them profound compassion, and who could have become the most effective ministers if the church had helped them heal instead of shaming them for hurting.

We are losing the questioners—people brave enough to ask hard questions about faith and suffering, who could have deepened the church's theology if we had welcomed their doubts instead of treating them as threats.

We are losing the young—people who have grown up with more awareness of mental health than any previous generation, who will not accept "pray harder" as the answer to psychological wounds.

We are losing the children of those who left—because when wounded people leave, they take their kids with them, and those kids grow up outside the church, often inheriting their parents' pain and distance from faith.

And we are losing our credibility. Every person who leaves wounded tells others about their experience. Every failure to help becomes a story that spreads. The church's reputation as a place of healing is being replaced with a reputation as a place of harm—not because we intend harm, but because our blindness produces it.

The Acceleration

Here is what makes this urgent: The exodus is accelerating.

Research shows that Generation Z has the highest ACE rates in history.[4] A whopping 76% of current high school students report one or more ACEs, compared to 64% reported by adults in earlier CDC surveys. The generation entering adulthood now carries more childhood trauma than any generation before them.

And they are the least churched generation in American history.

This is not coincidence. A generation with unprecedented trauma rates is walking away from institutions they perceive as unable to help with that trauma. They have seen the church fail their parents. They have heard the stories. They have learned that "pray harder" is not the answer.

If the church does not learn to address trauma, we will lose this generation entirely—not to secularism, but to pain. They will conclude that the church has nothing to offer for their actual wounds. And they may be right—unless we change.

And then something unexpected happened.

The Window That Just Opened

In the fall of 2025, following the assassination of Turning Point USA co-founder Charlie Kirk—a young leader known for his vocal Christian faith—churches across the country reported a sudden surge in attendance, particularly among young adults. Pastors in Pennsylvania, Ohio, Michigan, Illinois, and Colorado described young people walking through their doors who had not attended a service in years.[5] Bible sales surged. A Barna Group study found that Gen Z Christians were now attending church more frequently than any other generation—nearly twice a month on average, rates that had doubled since 2020.[6]

Whatever one thinks of the politics surrounding that moment, the phenomenon itself is unmistakable: a generation that had walked away from church started walking back in.

This should fill church leaders with both hope and terror.

Hope, because it means the hunger is still there. Young people are not done with faith. They are searching for meaning, for transcendence, for the very things McKinsey's researchers found essential to human flourishing. Something in them still responds to the call of the gospel.

Terror, because these young people are the most traumatized generation in American history. 76% of them carry ACEs. They are walking through your doors with nervous systems shaped by childhood adversity, brains wired for threat detection, and an acute sensitivity to institutional environments that do not feel safe.

If they walk back into churches that are still saying "pray harder"—churches that still cannot see trauma, still confuse neurobiological injury with spiritual failure, still offer wellness programs designed for intact nervous systems—they will leave again. And this time, they will not come back.

You have been given a second chance. The generation you were losing is showing up again. The question is not whether they will come. They are already coming. The question is whether you will be ready—whether you will have anything to offer them besides the same approach that drove their parents away.

This window will not stay open forever.

The Numbers Behind the Names

Let me put some numbers to these stories.

Consider a typical congregation of 2,000 members. Based on what we know about ACE prevalence:

Approximately 1,401 of those members carry unresolved childhood trauma—65% of your congregation, bleeding invisibly in the pews.

Of those 1,400, roughly 400 have ACE scores of 4 or higher—the threshold where risk of depression more than triples, suicide attempts increase nearly tenfold, and addiction becomes dramatically more likely.

In that same congregation, approximately 220 members are currently struggling with depression serious enough to affect their daily functioning. Another 180 are dealing with anxiety disorders. Perhaps 50 are contemplating suicide at this very moment—though you would never know it from their Sunday morning smiles.

Here is the number that should keep church leaders awake at night: of the new visitors who walk through your doors this year—people actively seeking a church home—the majority will leave within six months if they do not find what they are looking for.

What are they looking for?

Healing.

And if all you offer is, "Pray harder," they will find the door.

Yet, there is something even more troubling than the people who leave: The people who stay but still quit.

The Quiet Quitting

Corporate researchers have documented a phenomenon called "quiet quitting"—employees who remain in their jobs but mentally and emotionally disengage. They show up, do the minimum, and check out. They have quit without leaving.

Churches are full of quiet quitters.

They sit in the pews every Sunday. They smile when expected. They sing when prompted. They shake hands in the lobby and say "fine" when asked how they are doing.

But inside, they stopped hoping years ago. They stopped expecting the church to help with their real struggles. They stopped sharing how they're really doing. They stopped believing that anyone in the building could see their wounds or offer effective treatment.

They are still there. But they are not really there.

In some ways, this is worse than leaving. At least the people who leave have acknowledged the disconnect. The quiet quitters exist in a kind of spiritual purgatory—going through the motions of faith while the actual substance of it drains away.

And their children watch. They see parents who attend church but do not seem transformed by it. They observe the gap between what church claims to offer and what it actually delivers. And they decide, often unconsciously, that if this is all there is—if church cannot even help mom and dad—then why bother?

The exodus is not just about who leaves. It is about who stays but disappears.

What Could Be Different

But imagine the alternative.

Imagine a church known for actually healing people. Not just talking about healing, but actually producing it. A church where people with anxiety find relief. Where people with depression find hope. Where people with trauma find understanding and effective help.

Imagine word spreading: "That church helped me when nothing else worked." Imagine the wounded seeking it out: "I heard they actually know what to do with trauma." Imagine the young people showing up right now—the ones searching, the ones grieving, the ones hungry for something real—finding a church that actually knows how to hold their pain.

Imagine the exodus reversing—not because the church marketed itself better or made worship more entertaining, but because it became what Jesus intended: a place where the brokenhearted are bound up. Where the captives are set free. Where the prisoners find release.

This is not fantasy. This is what becomes possible when churches become trauma-responsive.

The bleeding in the pews does not have to continue. The exodus does not have to accelerate. The window that just opened does not have to close. The church can change.

But first, we need to see the full scope of what blindness is costing. The exodus is just the beginning. In the next chapter, we will look at another hemorrhage—one that claims lives, destroys families, and has hidden in plain sight for decades. The addiction crisis the church does not see.

Endnotes

1. Gallup, "Religion," Gallup Historical Trends, accessed 2024, https://news.gallup.com/poll/1690/religion.aspx.

2. Jeffrey M. Jones, "U.S. Church Membership Falls Below Majority for First Time," Gallup, March 29, 2021, https://news.gallup.com/poll/341963/church-membership-falls-below-majority-first-time.aspx.

3. Pew Research Center, "In U.S., Decline of Christianity Continues at Rapid Pace," October 17, 2019, https://www.pewresearch.org/religion/2019/10/17/in-u-s-decline-of-christianity-continues-at-rapid-pace/.

4. E. A. Swedo et al., "Adverse Childhood Experiences and Health Conditions and Risk Behaviors Among High School Students—Youth Risk Behavior Survey, United States, 2023," *MMWR Supplements* 73, no. Suppl-4 (2024): 39–49.

5. J. P. De Gance, quoted in "Church Attendance Rising After Charlie Kirk's Assassination," *The Christian Post*, September 28, 2025, https://www.christianpost.com/news/church-attendance-rising-after-charlie-kirks-assassination.html. Communio ministry, tracking attendance data across 400 churches nationwide.

6. Barna Group, "New Barna Data: Young Adults Lead a Resurgence in Church Attendance," Barna Group, October 14, 2025, https://www.barna.com/research/young-adults-lead-re

surgence-in-church-attendance/. Data based on 5,580 online interviews conducted January–July 2025.

Chapter Ten

The Addiction Crisis the Church Doesn't See

> "Addiction is as normal a response to trauma as bleeding is to being cut."
>
> –Michael Menard

I LOST TWO BROTHERS to heroin.

Adam and Patrick. Two of the funniest, most charming people you would ever meet. The kind of guys who lit up a room just by walking into it. People loved them. I loved them.

And for years, I watched them destroy themselves—watched their bodies deteriorate, watched their potential evaporate, watched them lie and steal and disappear for months at a time. I watched my parents age a decade in a year from the stress of it. I watched family gatherings become minefields of tension and grief and desperate hope that maybe this time would be different.

It was never different. Not until they were gone.

For most of those years, I thought what everyone thinks about addicts. That they were weak. That they were making bad choices. That if they just tried harder, prayed more, had more willpower, they could stop. I loved them, but I also judged them. How could they keep doing this to themselves? To us?

It was not until I started researching childhood trauma for my memoir that I finally understood. Adam and Patrick were not weak. They were wounded. They were not making bad choices. They were self-medicating unbearable pain with the only thing that worked. They were not morally deficient. They were wounded by the same childhood that wounded me—except their wound expressed itself through addiction while mine expressed itself through workaholism and performance.

Same wound. Different symptoms.

What the Wound Looked Like

We grew up in a family of 14 children in Kankakee, Illinois. Fourteen kids. One house. Not enough of anything—not enough space, not enough money, not enough calm, not enough attention to go around. The chaos was constant. You learned early to fend for yourself, to read the room for danger, to disappear when things got bad.

Adam and Patrick were in the middle of the pack—old enough to see everything, young enough to have no power over any of it. They watched the same dysfunction I did. They absorbed the same fear, the same unpredictability, the same message that the world was not safe and the people who were supposed to protect you could not always be counted on.

But here is what I did not understand until decades later: we did not all metabolize that chaos the same way. I turned mine into drive. I became the achiever, the inventor, the one who would control his environment through sheer competence. My nervous system said: *if I perform well enough, I will be safe.* Adam and Patrick's nervous systems found a different answer: *if I can just make this pain stop, I will survive.*

Both were survival strategies. Mine was rewarded. Theirs was condemned.

The church we knew growing up did not have language for any of this. When Adam started using, the response was what you would expect from good people who did not know what they were dealing with. *Pray for him. He needs to get right with God. He is choosing this.* When Patrick followed the same path—because trauma runs in families and so does the search for relief—the church doubled down. Two brothers, same sin, same weakness, same failure to surrender.

Nobody asked what happened in that house. Nobody connected 14 children and not enough of anything to two boys who found heroin in their twenties. Nobody understood that the substances were not the disease. They were the medication.

What I Wish I Had Known

After Patrick died, I was angry. Not at him—at myself. At all of us. At every system that had touched their lives and failed to see what was underneath.

After I found the ACE research, the anger turned into something worse: clarity. I could trace the line from our childhood to their graves with scientific precision. The dose-response curve. The neurobiological damage. The predictable, measurable, preventable progression from childhood adversity to adult addiction to early death.

If I knew back then what I know now, my brothers would still be with me.

That sentence haunts me. It is the reason I am writing this book. It is the reason I founded United Against Childhood Trauma (UACT). It is the reason I will not stop until every church, every school, every organization in America understands what childhood trauma actually does to a human being—because the cost of not understanding is measured in bodies. And two of those bodies were my brothers.

This chapter is for everyone who has watched someone they love disappear into addiction. It is for everyone who has struggled with addiction themselves and wondered why they could not just stop. It is for every church that has prayed over addicts, counseled addicts, buried addicts—and never understood what they were actually dealing with.

Because here is what the science now proves beyond any doubt: addiction is not a moral failure. It is the predictable neurobiological consequence of childhood trauma.

The Numbers That Change Everything

Let me give you the data that rewrote everything I thought I knew about addiction.

Between 56 and 67% of all adult illicit drug use is directly attributable to Adverse Childhood Experiences.[1] Not correlated with. Attributable to. That is the same methodology that proved smoking causes lung cancer. We are talking about causation, not coincidence.

A shocking 63% of injection drug use—the kind that killed my brothers—is attributable to childhood trauma.[2]

Among adolescents, the numbers are even more devastating. About 70 to 84% of opioid misuse among teenagers is attributable to ACEs.[3] That means if we prevented childhood trauma, we would prevent up to 84% of the teenage opioid crisis.

The relationship follows what researchers call a dose-response pattern. The more trauma, the more addiction. Adults with four or more ACEs are four times more likely to develop alcohol-related disorders.[4]

Individuals with six or more ACEs are 11.3 times more likely to use injection drugs.[5]

Not four times, not ten times—11.3 times more likely.

This is not a risk factor. This is a cause.

Why Substances "Work"

Here is what I did not understand about Adam and Patrick until it was too late: they were not using heroin to get high. They were using heroin to feel normal.

When children experience trauma, their developing brains are flooded with cortisol—the stress hormone. This is not a brief spike that resolves. In traumatized children, cortisol levels remain elevated for years, sometimes decades. Too much, for too long.[6]

This chronic cortisol exposure physically damages the developing brain. The amygdala—the fear center—becomes hyperactivated, stuck in permanent alarm mode. The prefrontal cortex—responsible for judgment, impulse control, and decision-making—under develops. The hippocampus—which regulates stress and memory—actually shrinks.[7]

The result? Anxiety that never stops. Depression that descends without warning. An inability to regulate emotions. Chronic psychological pain that most people cannot even imagine.

And then someone offers you something that makes it stop.

Traumatized individuals do not randomly choose substances. They unconsciously select drugs that temporarily correct their specific neurobiological deficits.

Opioids replace depleted endorphins. They provide the warmth and comfort that was absent in childhood. They temporarily silence emotional pain that has been screaming for years.

Alcohol reduces amygdala hyperactivity. It temporarily decreases the anxiety that never stops. It numbs the hypervigilance that comes from years of living in fear.

Stimulants compensate for prefrontal cortex damage. They improve focus that was disrupted by trauma. They provide energy depleted by years of cellular exhaustion.

The cruel irony is that substances that initially correct trauma-induced deficits ultimately worsen them. Tolerance develops, requiring increasing doses. Withdrawal recreates the original trauma symptoms. The brain adapts, deepening the neurobiological dysfunction. The "solution" becomes the problem.

But by then, the trap has closed.

Ethan

Ethan grew up in what looked like the perfect Christian home. His father was an elder. His mother led the choir. They attended church three times a week and hosted the youth group in their basement.

What no one saw: Ethan's father was a different man at home. Rage that erupted without warning. Criticism that cut to the bone. Physical "discipline" that crossed lines no child should experience. And through it all, the demand for perfect behavior, perfect grades, perfect faith—or else.

Ethan performed perfectly. He had no choice.

He went to a Christian college, majored in business, got a job at a reputable firm. He married a woman from church. He taught Sunday school. He looked exactly like a successful Christian young man should look like.

He also drank alone every night after his wife went to bed. Just enough to quiet the anxiety that never stopped. Just enough to silence the voice in his head that still sounded like his father, still told him he was worthless, still made him feel like a terrified child no matter how much success he achieved.

Over years, "just enough" became more. And more. His wife found bottles hidden in the garage. His work performance slipped. He started missing church—too hungover on Sunday mornings, too ashamed to face people who thought he had it all together.

When he finally confessed to his pastor, the response was what you would expect: "You need to repent of this sin. You need to surrender it to God. You need to trust Him for victory."

Ethan tried. God knows he tried. He went to the altar. He joined the men's accountability group. He prayed every morning for strength to resist. He memorized verses about self-control.

And every night, he drank. Because willpower cannot overcome neurobiological damage. Because prayer does not rewire a dysregulated nervous system. Because the pain that drove him to alcohol in the first place had never been addressed—only its symptom.

It took Ethan three more years—and a DUI that nearly destroyed his career—before he found a therapist who understood trauma. In their first session, she asked a question no one in his church had ever asked: "What happened to you as a child?"

That question changed everything. Not immediately. Healing from trauma takes time. But for the first time, Ethan understood that his drinking was not a spiritual failure. It was an attempt to survive wounds no one had ever helped him heal.

What the Church Has Done And What It Has Missed

Let me be honest about something. The church has not been entirely blind to addiction. In many ways, it has been more willing to engage with addiction than with almost any other expression of trauma.

Celebrate Recovery—a Christ-centered recovery program born out of Saddleback Church—now operates in more than 35,000 churches worldwide. Alcoholics Anonymous, which was founded on spiritual principles, holds meetings in church basements across America. Many congregations have developed partnerships with local treatment centers, hired counselors with addiction expertise, and created recovery ministries that offer genuine community and accountability.

These efforts matter. They have saved lives. They represent the church at its best—showing up for people in crisis, opening its doors when other institutions closed theirs, refusing to abandon the struggling even when progress was slow and relapse was frequent.

I honor that work. I am not dismissing it.

But here is what even the best recovery programs in the church have largely missed. They treat addiction as the primary problem. They focus on sobriety as the goal. They build accountability structures around the substance use. And while they often acknowledge that pain drives addiction, they rarely have the tools or training to address the underlying trauma that created that pain in the first place.

Celebrate Recovery's 12 steps include a powerful inventory process and a reliance on God's power. But 12 steps designed for healthy adults who developed unhealthy habits work differently for traumatized adults whose neurobiological wiring makes steps like "make a searching and fearless moral inventory" potentially retraumatizing. Asking a trauma survivor to catalog their moral failures before addressing the wounds that produced those failures can deepen shame rather than relieve it.

AA meetings in church basements create vital community. But community alone does not rewire a dysregulated nervous system. You can attend meetings every day for a decade and still be white-knuckling sobriety because the cortisol is still flooding, the amygdala is still firing, and the pain that started in childhood is still screaming for relief.

The church's recovery efforts are not wrong. They are incomplete. They address the symptom with courage and compassion. But they leave the wound untreated. And untreated wounds do not heal—they fester. Which is why relapse rates remain so stubbornly high even among people in strong recovery communities.

The next step is not to abandon what the church has built. It is to add what has been missing: trauma-responsive care that addresses the root cause, not just the visible behavior.

The Opioid Crisis Is a Trauma Crisis

Let me put this in perspective.

In 2022, over 110,000 Americans died from drug overdoses.[8] That is more than car accidents, gun violence, and HIV combined. It is roughly 300 people every single day—a plane crash worth of deaths, every day, with no end in sight.

We call this the "opioid crisis" or the "drug epidemic." We talk about it as if it is primarily a problem of supply—too many pills, too much fentanyl, too many dealers.

But the opioid crisis is fundamentally a trauma crisis. The demand exists because millions of traumatized Americans are desperate for relief from pain that nothing else touches. Cut off the supply, and they find another source. Remove one drug, and they switch to another. The market exists because the wound exists.

Conservatively, 60% of those 110,000 overdose deaths—66,000 Americans—died from what is fundamentally a childhood trauma problem.[9] That's 66,000 people who might still be alive if someone had addressed their trauma instead of just treating their addiction.

Many of those people sat in church pews. Many of them came forward for prayer. Many of them went through recovery programs that helped them get sober but never helped them get healed. Many of them died believing they had failed God, when really the systems around them had failed to see their wound.

The Intergenerational Cycle

Here is what makes addiction so devastating: it perpetuates itself across generations.

Traumatized children grow into wounded adults. Wounded adults often self-medicate with substances. Addicted adults create chaotic, unpredictable, sometimes abusive homes. Children in those homes experience trauma. Those traumatized children grow up and self-medicate. The cycle continues.

76% of child abuse is perpetrated by parents.[10] Parents who were often themselves abused. Parents who often struggle with addiction. Parents who are not monsters—they are wounded people wounding the next generation because no one ever helped them heal.

Adam and Patrick grew up in the same home I did. We experienced the same chaos, the same fear, the same wounds. I found my escape through achievement and control. They found theirs through substances. But all three of us were responding to the same trauma.

Both of my brothers had children before they died. And the cycle continued. One of Patrick's sons became a heroin addict himself because Patrick introduced him to the drug. Think about that. A father so captured by his own wound that he passed the instrument of his destruction to his own child. Not because he was evil. Because he was sick. Because addiction is a disease that consumes everything, including parental judgment, including love itself.

The cycle would have continued further if left unchecked. Not because Adam or Patrick were bad people. Because trauma begets trauma until someone breaks the chain.

Rachel

Rachel never touched alcohol or drugs. Her father's addiction had shown her where that road led, and she was determined never to walk it.

Instead, she found church. Found Jesus. Found a community that became the family her biological family had never been. She threw herself into ministry—youth group, women's Bible study, missions trips, prayer teams. If there was a need, Rachel was there.

What Rachel did not realize: she had simply traded one addiction for another. Her compulsive serving was self-medication too—a way to earn worth she had never felt, to stay busy enough that she did not have to feel the pain underneath, to prove that she was nothing like her father.

The church loved her for it. They praised her commitment. They held her up as an example. They never asked why a young woman would work herself to exhaustion week after week, why she could not say no to any request, why she seemed so driven by something that looked like faith but felt like desperation.

Rachel burned out at 32. Complete physical and emotional collapse. Could not get out of bed for a month. The anxiety and depression she had been outrunning for years finally caught up.

This might sound dramatic. It is not. This happens far more often than most people realize. Churches are full of Rachels—people whose compulsive serving looks like faithfulness but is actually self-medication. People running from wounds they have never faced. People who will eventually collapse because you cannot outrun what lives inside you.

In therapy, she learned something that rocked her understanding of herself: she was just like her father. Not because she drank—she did not drink. But because they were both trying to escape the same pain in different ways. He used heroin. She used religious performance. Same wound. Different drug.

The church had celebrated her addiction because it looked like faithfulness. They never saw the trauma driving it.

What Would Change

Imagine if churches took what they have already built—the recovery ministries, the accountability groups, the willingness to show up for people in crisis—and added trauma-responsive care to the foundation.

Instead of shame, they would offer understanding. Instead of "repent harder," they would ask "what happened to you?" Instead of treating substance use as the problem, they would recognize it as a symptom pointing to a deeper wound.

Recovery programs would still matter. Accountability would still matter. Celebrate Recovery's community and spiritual framework would still matter. But they would be supplemented by trained facilitators who understand trauma, by partnerships with therapists who can address neurobiological injury, by an organizational awareness that the person sitting in the recovery circle is not fundamentally different from the person sitting in the Sunday morning pew. They are both carrying wounds. One found substances. The other found something less visible.

Churches could train their recovery leaders to recognize trauma signs. They could create environments where addicts are not pariahs to be fixed but wounded people to be healed—just like everyone else in the pews who is coping with trauma in less visible ways. They could build on the extraordinary infrastructure they have already created and make it complete.

And maybe—just maybe—fewer people would die. Fewer families would be destroyed. Fewer children would grow up with addicted parents and continue the cycle.

This is not about being soft on addiction. It is about being effective. The current approach—treating addiction as primarily a moral and spiritual failure—has not worked well enough. The relapse rates prove it. The overdose numbers prove it. The families shattered by relapse after relapse prove it.

The church has already demonstrated the courage to engage. Now it needs the knowledge to heal.

For Those Still Bleeding

If you are reading this and you struggle with addiction, I want you to hear something that your church may never have told you.

You are not weak. You are wounded.

Your addiction is not evidence that you love your substance more than God. It is evidence that something happened to you that created pain you are trying to survive.

Your repeated failures are not proof that you are beyond hope. They are proof that the approaches you have been given do not address the actual problem.

There is help that works. Trauma-responsive treatment that addresses the root, not just the symptom. Therapy approaches like EMDR that can rewire the neurobiological damage driving your addiction. Communities that see your wound instead of just judging your behavior.

And yes, God is still with you. Not standing at a distance, arms crossed, waiting for you to get your act together. But right there in the pit with you, grieving over your pain, longing for your healing, offering resources you may not have known existed.

The same Jesus who touched lepers and ate with sinners and welcomed the broken is not ashamed of you. He sees the wound underneath the addiction. He knows what happened to you. And He wants you whole—not just sober, but healed.

My brothers never got that message. The church they knew had good people who loved them—but those good people did not have the knowledge to see past the behavior to the wound underneath. Adam and Patrick died believing they were failures.

They were not failures. They were casualties of a wound no one knew how to treat.

If I knew back then what I know now, my brothers would still be with me. I cannot change the past. But I can make sure that someone reading this—someone who loves an addict, someone who is an addict—knows the truth that could have saved Adam and Patrick.

You do not have to be another casualty.

But addiction is not the only way trauma hemorrhages through our congregations. In the next chapter, we will look at something even closer to home: the families sitting in your pews, struggling in ways you cannot see, carrying wounds that affect not only individuals but entire generations.

The families behind your members.

Endnotes

1. S. R. Dube et al., "Childhood Abuse, Household Dysfunction and the Risk of Illicit Drug Use," *Pediatrics* 111, no. 3 (2003): 564–572.

2. V. J. Felitti et al., "Relationship of Childhood Abuse and Household Dysfunction to Many of the Leading Causes of Death in Adults: The Adverse Childhood Experiences (ACE) Study," *American Journal of Preventive Medicine* 14, no. 4 (1998): 245–258.

3. A. E. Austin et al., "Adolescent Opioid Misuse Attributable to Adverse Childhood Experiences," *Journal of Pediatrics* 224 (2020): 102–109.

4. S. R. Dube et al., "Adverse Childhood Experiences and Personal Alcohol Abuse as an Adult," *Addictive Behaviors* 27 (2002): 713–725.

5. Felitti et al., "Relationship of Childhood Abuse," 245–258. Alcoholism: 3% for 0 ACEs vs 16% for 4+ ACEs (5.3x multiplier); IV drug use: 0.3% for 0 ACEs vs 3.4% for 4+ ACEs (11.3x multiplier).

6. Harvard Center on the Developing Child, "Toxic Stress," Harvard University, accessed 2023, https://developingchild.harvard.edu/key-concept/toxic-stress/.

7. M. H. Teicher, J. A. Samson, C. M. Anderson, and K. Ohashi, "The Effects of Childhood Maltreatment on Brain Structure,

Function and Connectivity," *Nature Reviews Neuroscience* 17, no. 10 (2016): 652–666, https://www.nature.com/articles/nrn.2016.111.

8. Merianne Rose Spencer, Melonie Heron Garnett, and Arialdi M. Miniño, "Drug Overdose Deaths in the United States, 2002–2022," NCHS Data Brief no. 491 (Hyattsville, MD: National Center for Health Statistics, 2024), https://www.cdc.gov/nchs/products/databriefs/db491.htm.

9. Author's conservative estimate based on CDC overdose data and ACE-attributable fraction research.

10. National Children's Alliance, "National Statistics on Child Abuse," 2024, https://www.nationalchildrensalliance.org/media-room/national-statistics-on-child-abuse/.

Chapter Eleven

The Families Behind Your Members

> "But if serving the Lord seems undesirable to you, then choose for yourselves this day whom you will serve . . . . But as for me and my household, we will serve the Lord."
>
> –Joshua 24:15

From the very beginning, God designed us for family.

It was not good for man to be alone, so God created partnership. Be fruitful and multiply, He commanded, establishing the family as the fundamental unit of human society. Honor your father and mother—the only commandment with a promise attached. Fathers, do not provoke your children to anger, but bring them up in the discipline and instruction of the Lord. Train up a child in the way he should go.

Scripture is saturated with family. God reveals Himself as Father. We are adopted as sons and daughters. The church is described as a household of faith. Marriage is held up as a picture of Christ and His bride. The Bible begins with a family in a garden and ends with a wedding feast.

Family matters to God. Which means what happens to families should matter desperately to His church.

And what is happening to families—what childhood trauma is doing to marriages, to parenting, to the generational transmission of faith itself—is a crisis hiding in plain sight.

The Room Where Everyone Sat Down

I was in a room with 300 people.

It was a book launch event, and I wanted to make the prevalence of childhood trauma tangible—not just statistics on a page, but something people could feel in the room. So I asked everyone to stand.

Three hundred people rose to their feet. Young and old. Men and women. Business executives and stay-at-home parents. Church leaders and people who had not been to church in years.

Then I made a simple request: "If you have experienced childhood trauma, or if you know someone close to you who has—a spouse, a child, a parent, a sibling, a close friend—please take a seat."

Every single person sat down.

Immediately.

I have repeated this exercise five times now with different groups. The result is always the same. In a statistically significant sample, childhood trauma touches everyone—either directly or through someone they love.

The mathematics explains why.

The Mathematics of Universal Impact

We have established that approximately 70% of adults have experienced at least one Adverse Childhood Experience. That means 30% have not.

But here is what those numbers actually mean for families.

The probability that any single person escaped childhood trauma is 30%, or 0.30. In a two-person relationship—a marriage, a partnership—the probability that both people escaped trauma is 0.30 times 0.30, which equals 0.09, or 9%.

This means 91% of couples include at least one person carrying childhood trauma.

Extend this to a typical household of three people—two parents and a child, or two adults and a roommate, or a single parent with two children. The probability that all three escaped trauma is 0.30 times 0.30 times 0.30, which equals 0.027, or just 2.7%.

This means 97.3% of households contain at least one person who has experienced childhood trauma.

Read that again—97% of households.

This is why everyone in that room of 300 sat down. This is why childhood trauma is not a problem affecting "some people." This is why, even if you personally escaped childhood adversity, you are almost certainly living with, loving, working alongside, or raising someone who did not.

Childhood trauma affects us all. Every single one of us. The question is not whether it touches your life, but how.

To understand that "how," I want to introduce you to one family. Their story will carry us through the rest of this chapter, because what happened to them is not unusual. It is the pattern that plays out in millions of homes, including homes in your congregation.

The Caldwells

Ruth Caldwell grew up in rural Kentucky in the 1960s. Her father drank. Her mother coped by disappearing—not physically, but emotionally. She was present in the house but absent in every way that mattered. Ruth learned early that she was on her own. No one was coming to help. No one would notice if she was hurting. The world was something you endured, not something you enjoyed.

Ruth married young—at 18—because marriage was what you did, and because a boy named Dale paid attention to her, and attention felt like love when you had never had enough of either. Dale was a decent man, but he had his own wounds: a father who never showed affection, a mother who demanded perfection, a childhood that taught him emotions are weakness. He worked hard. He provided. He did not know how to be close.

They attended church every Sunday. They raised three children. From the outside, they looked like exactly the kind of solid Christian family your congregation celebrates.

From the inside, their home was cold. Not violent. Not chaotic. Just empty. Ruth's depression—undiagnosed, untreated, unacknowledged—hung over the household like a fog. Dale's emotional unavailability meant the children grew up in a home where needs were met physically but not emotionally. They were fed, clothed, sheltered, and profoundly alone.

Their middle daughter, Grace, absorbed all of it. And she carried it into everything that came after.

How Trauma Transmits Across Generations

Before I tell you what happened to Grace, I need to explain how trauma moves from parent to child. Because it does not happen the way most people think. It is not simply that bad parents produce bad children. The transmission is more subtle than that, more insidious, and it operates through at least five distinct pathways—often simultaneously.

Attachment disruption. This is the most fundamental pathway. Children are born with an innate need to attach to a primary caregiver. When that caregiver is emotionally available, responsive, and consistent, the child develops what psychologists call secure attachment—the internal sense that the world is safe, that relationships are trustworthy, that they are worthy of love.[1] But when the caregiver is depressed, anxious, dissociated, or emotionally unavailable—as traumatized parents often are—the child's attachment system develops differently. They learn that love is unreliable, that they must earn connection, that closeness is dangerous. These attachment patterns do not disappear when the child grows up. They become the template for every relationship that follows—friendships, marriages, parenting, even their relationship with God.

Modeling of dysregulation. Children's nervous systems are not self-regulating at birth. They learn to regulate—to calm down, to manage emotions, to move between states of arousal and rest—by being co-regulated by their caregivers.[2] A parent who can stay calm when a child is distressed teaches that child's nervous system how to find calm. But a parent whose own nervous system is chronically dysregulated—stuck in fight, flight, or freeze from their own unresolved trauma—cannot model what they do not have. The child's developing nervous system calibrates to the parent's dysregulated state. They absorb the anxiety, the reactivity, and the emotional volatility. Not because anyone teaches it to them, but because their biology is designed to mirror the biology of the person closest to them.

Epigenetic changes. This is perhaps the most sobering pathway. Research in the emerging field of epigenetics has shown that extreme stress and trauma can alter gene expression—not by changing the DNA itself, but by modifying how genes are activated or silenced.[3] Studies of Holocaust survivors, famine victims, and other populations exposed to extreme adversity have found epigenetic markers that were passed to their children and, in some cases, their grandchildren. This means trauma can leave biological fingerprints that transmit across generations before the child is even born. The implications are staggering: some children may inherit a biological predisposition to anxiety, depression, or heightened stress reactivity not because of their own experiences, but because of what happened to their parents or grandparents.

Learned coping patterns. Children learn how to cope with stress, conflict, and emotional pain by watching their parents. If a parent copes by drinking, the child learns that substances are how you manage pain. If a parent copes by withdrawing emotionally, the child learns that shutting down is how you survive. If a parent copes by erupting in rage, the child learns that anger is the acceptable outlet for distress. If a parent copes through religious performance—compulsive serving, rigid rule-following, spiritual busyness—the child learns that faith is about earning safety rather than receiving grace. These patterns are not consciously taught. They are absorbed through daily observation over thousands of interactions across years of development.

Environmental factors. Traumatized parents often create—without intending to—environments that replicate the conditions of their own childhood. The parent who grew up in chaos may create chaos through their own instability, addiction, or relational dysfunction. The parent who grew up in rigid control may create a home characterized by the same suffocating perfectionism. The parent who grew up in poverty may struggle to provide stability because their own capacity to earn and manage resources was compromised by the effects of their childhood adversity. The environment becomes the vehicle through which trauma travels, even when the parent's conscious intention is to do better.

These five pathways rarely operate in isolation. In most trauma-affected families, they compound one another—attachment disruption making the child vulnerable, dysregulation modeling teaching them unhealthy patterns, epigenetic changes predisposing their biology, learned coping giving them the wrong tools, and environmental factors surrounding them with the conditions for the cycle to continue.

This is what was happening in the Caldwell home. Ruth's depression created an environment of emotional absence. Her inability to regulate her own grief and anxiety meant her children never learned to regulate theirs. Grace watched her mother endure rather than engage, withdraw rather than connect, perform faith rather than experience it. And Grace's developing attachment system recorded all of it.

What Trauma Does to Marriage

Grace Caldwell married Nathan at 23. He was everything her father was not—warm, expressive, emotionally present. She fell in love with him precisely because he offered what she had never had: someone who actually wanted to be close.

What Grace did not understand was that she had no template for receiving what Nathan offered. Closeness felt dangerous. Vulnerability triggered the part of her nervous system that had learned, growing up with Ruth, that depending on someone's emotional presence was a setup for disappointment. So Grace did the thing that made no conscious sense but made perfect neurobiological sense: she pushed Nathan away.[4]

Not dramatically. Not cruelly. She just retreated. When Nathan tried to connect, she found reasons to be busy. When he expressed affection, she deflected. When conflict arose, she shut down completely—the same way her mother had, the same emotional disappearing act she had absorbed in a thousand daily moments across her childhood.

Nathan, confused and hurt by the distance he could not understand, did what his own childhood had taught him. His father had been critical and demanding. Nathan had learned that when something was not working, the answer was to try harder, push more, fix the problem. He pursued Grace—not with rage, but with relentless intensity. More conversations. More questions. More attempts to break through the wall she had built.

His pursuit felt to Grace exactly like the thing she feared most: someone demanding emotional access she could not provide. She retreated further. He pursued harder. The distance grew.

Their pastor, when they finally went for help, tried the standard approaches. Communication techniques. Love languages. Date nights. These helped marginally, but the pattern kept recurring, because the pattern was not a communication problem. It was two trauma responses colliding.

Grace's nervous system interpreted closeness as danger because her earliest experience of closeness—with her mother—taught her that the people closest to you are the ones most likely to disappear. Nathan's nervous system interpreted distance as failure because his earliest experience—with his demanding father—taught him that if things were not working, it was because he was not trying hard enough.

Their marriage was not failing because they had chosen poorly or loved inadequately. Their marriage was failing because two wounded people were triggering each other's deepest fears without knowing it. Each was reacting not to their actual spouse but to ghosts from their childhoods.

This is the pattern in trauma-affected marriages. The fight about money is often really about control—because someone who grew up in chaos desperately needs to control something to feel safe. The fight about in-laws is often really about loyalty—because someone who was never protected as a child needs to know their spouse will choose them. The fight about sex is often really about safety—because physical intimacy requires vulnerability, and vulnerability feels dangerous to someone whose body learned early on that it was not their own.

Pastors and marriage counselors who do not understand trauma will address the surface issue and wonder why it keeps coming back. They will teach communication skills to people whose nervous systems are too activated to use them. They will encourage vulnerability to people for whom vulnerability has always meant pain. They will tell couples to "just forgive" when the real work is healing wounds that make forgiveness feel impossible.

The question that changes everything is the question almost no one asks: "What happened to you?"

What Trauma Does to Parenting

Grace and Nathan had two children: a son, Tyler, and a daughter, Sophie.

Grace loved her children fiercely—with a love she was determined would look nothing like what she had received from Ruth. She would be present. She would be warm. She would be everything her mother was not.

But the body does not follow the will's instructions when the nervous system is running programs written in childhood. Grace could not give her children what she had never received herself. She tried—God knows she tried—but in moments of stress, exhaustion, or overwhelm, her system defaulted to what it knew. She withdrew. She went quiet. She was physically in the room but emotionally somewhere else. The same fog Ruth had created was now settling over a new generation.

Tyler, the older child, responded the way Nathan had: by trying harder. He became the good kid, the helper, the one who monitored his mother's mood and adjusted his behavior to keep the peace. At eight years old, he was parenting his parent—a role reversal that psychologists call parentification, one of the most common and least recognized forms of childhood trauma.

Sophie responded differently. Where Tyler performed, Sophie protested. She had tantrums that seemed disproportionate. She clung to Grace at drop-off, screamed when Grace left the room, and could not self-soothe in moments of distress. She was not "difficult." She was communicating—in the only language a young child has—that her attachment system was insecure. She could not trust that her mother would be emotionally available, so she escalated to ensure proximity. Her nervous system had already learned, at four years old, what Ruth's depression had taught Grace thirty years earlier: the people closest to you might disappear.

Nathan, meanwhile, overcompensated. Seeing Grace's withdrawal, he threw himself into parenting with the same intensity he brought to everything—managing, directing, correcting, fixing. He loved his children, but his love felt to them like pressure. Tyler performed harder. Sophie resisted more. The household became a system of unspoken tension, each member playing a role scripted by wounds that predated all of them.

This is what trauma does to parenting. It is not about bad intentions. Grace and Nathan wanted desperately to be good parents. They read the books. They attended the church parenting class. They prayed over their children every night.

But you cannot give what you do not have. You cannot model emotional regulation you never learned. You cannot create secure attachment from an insecure foundation. You cannot teach your children that the world is safe when your own nervous system is screaming that it is not.

The most loving parents in your congregation may be unknowingly transmitting their wounds to their children—not through abuse or neglect in any obvious sense, but through the subtle, daily, cumulative impact of a dysregulated nervous system on a developing one. The fog that settled over Ruth's house settled over Grace's house, too. Different furniture. Same weather.

When Children Need New Families

When Tyler was 14 and Sophie was 10, Grace and Nathan's marriage finally collapsed. The distance had become unbearable. Nathan had an affair—not because he stopped loving Grace, but because someone else offered the emotional connection Grace could not provide. Grace, devastated, descended into the same depression that had claimed her mother. For the first time in their lives, the household became truly unsafe.

Sophie was removed by child protective services and placed in foster care. Tyler went to live with Nathan's parents. I am telling you this not because the Caldwell story is extreme, but because it is common. A study of nearly three thousand children in Kansas's foster care system found that almost every child entering care had already lived through at least two adverse childhood experiences, and that close to eight in ten had lived through six or more.[5] These are not children who had one hard year. These are children who arrive carrying an accumulated lifetime of injury before anyone has met them.

Sophie arrived at her foster home carrying four generations of trauma: Ruth's childhood wounds that became Ruth's depression, that became Grace's attachment disruption, that became a marriage that collapsed, that became a ten-year-old girl sitting in a stranger's living room with a garbage bag of belongings and a nervous system wired for threat.

This is where the church has an extraordinary opportunity—and an extraordinary responsibility.

Christian families foster and adopt at rates significantly higher than the general population. Many churches actively encourage foster care as a ministry. And they should. These children need families. They need love. They need stability.

But love alone is not enough. And this is the part that many well-meaning foster and adoptive families—and the churches that support them—do not understand.

Sophie's foster parents, a kind couple from their church, were prepared for a "difficult" child. They were not prepared for the reality of trauma. Sophie's behaviors—the rages, the hoarding of food, the inability to accept affection, the lying about things that did not matter, the nighttime terrors—were not discipline problems. They were survival strategies developed across multiple generations of unaddressed trauma.

When her foster parents tried to hug her, Sophie stiffened. Not because she did not want comfort, but because physical closeness had never been safe. When they set boundaries, she escalated—not out of defiance, but because her nervous system interpreted authority as threat. When they praised her, she sabotaged herself—because she had learned that good things do not last and it is better to destroy them yourself than to wait for the inevitable loss.

Without training in trauma-responsive care, foster families burn out. Placements fail. Children are moved from home to home, each disruption confirming what their nervous systems already believe: *people leave, people cannot be trusted, I am not worth keeping.*

Churches that encourage foster care without equipping families for trauma are setting both the families and the children up for failure. They are sending soldiers into battle without armor. The intention is beautiful. The preparation is inadequate.

What would change if churches provided trauma-responsive training for every foster and adoptive family in their congregation? If they understood that a child with an ACE score of 5 needs more than a loving home—they need a home where the parents understand dysregulation, where the response to a meltdown is co-regulation rather than punishment, where the goal is not compliance but connection?

What would change if the church saw foster care not just as a compassion ministry but as a front line in breaking the intergenerational cycle of trauma?

As For Me and My Household

Joshua stood before the people of Israel and issued a challenge: "Choose this day whom you will serve." And then he made his own commitment clear: "As for me and my household, we will serve the Lord."

That commitment—"me and my household"—recognized something essential. Faith is not just individual. It is familial. What happens in our homes shapes what happens in our hearts, and vice versa. The household is the primary context in which faith is transmitted, tested, and lived out.

But childhood trauma disrupts that transmission. When parents are drowning in their own unhealed wounds, they struggle to pass on the faith they genuinely hold. When marriages are locked in trauma-driven conflict, children learn that love is painful rather than safe. When the home is a place of anxiety rather than peace, it becomes hard to believe in a God who offers rest.

Here is the hope that makes all of this worth confronting: The cycle can be broken.

Imagine if someone had helped Ruth—if her church had seen the depression behind the Sunday smile and connected her with real treatment. Grace might have grown up with a mother who was present. She might have developed secure attachment. She might have brought that security into her marriage rather than the fog she inherited.

Imagine if someone had helped Grace and Nathan—if their pastor had asked "what happened to you as children?" instead of prescribing date nights. They might have understood the ghosts driving their conflict. They might have healed together instead of destroying each other slowly.

Imagine if someone had helped Tyler and Sophie before the collapse—if the church had recognized that a withdrawn mother and an intense father were not just "having a rough patch" but were replaying intergenerational patterns that needed intervention.

Every chain of intergenerational trauma was broken by someone. Somewhere in every healthy family's history, there was a person who inherited wounds and refused to pass them on. They did not always have the language we have now. They did not know about ACEs or attachment theory or nervous system regulation. But somehow, through grace and grit and often through faith, they became what researchers call a "cycle breaker."

Imagine if the church equipped people to be cycle breakers intentionally rather than accidentally.

Imagine marriage counseling that starts with "What happened to each of you?" Imagine parenting classes that help trauma survivors understand how their wounds might affect their children—and what to do about it. Imagine premarital counseling that includes ACE assessments, helping couples understand what they are each bringing into the marriage before the patterns get entrenched. Imagine foster and adoptive parent training that prepares families for the reality of trauma-affected children rather than leaving them to discover it through crisis.

Imagine a church that sees family ministry not as programming for different age groups, but as the sacred work of healing generations.

The church that wants to fulfill the Great Commission must care about what is happening in households. Not just individual souls, but family systems. Not just Sunday attendance, but Monday morning breakfast tables. Not just sermons heard, but patterns lived.

Because the people bleeding in your pews do not bleed alone. They bleed into their marriages. They bleed into their parenting. They bleed into the next generation.

Ruth bled into Grace. Grace bled into Tyler and Sophie. Sophie bled into a foster system that struggles to hold children it does not understand.

Ruth sat in a church pew every Sunday of her childhood, bleeding invisibly, while no one asked what was happening at home.

Until the church learns to see families—really see them, with all their hidden wounds and intergenerational patterns—the hemorrhage will continue.

We have now seen the hemorrhage in its fullness: the exodus of the wounded, the addiction crisis driven by trauma, the families caught in cycles they do not understand.

The question that remains is: what do we do about it?

In Part Four, we will turn from diagnosis to prescription. From seeing the wound to binding it up. From understanding the crisis to becoming the solution.

The path from trauma-blind to trauma-responsive.

Endnotes

1. John Bowlby, *Attachment and Loss*, vol. 1, *Attachment* (New York: Basic Books, 1969).

2. Daniel J. Siegel and Mary Hartzell, *Parenting from the Inside Out: How a Deeper Self-Understanding Can Help You Raise Children Who Thrive* (New York: Tarcher, 2003).

3. R. Yehuda et al., "Influences of Maternal and Paternal PTSD on Epigenetic Regulation of the Glucocorticoid Receptor Gene in Holocaust Survivor Offspring," *American Journal of Psychiatry* 171, no. 8 (2014): 872–880.

4. Susan M. Johnson, *Hold Me Tight: Seven Conversations for a Lifetime of Love* (New York: Little, Brown, 2008).

5. Kelly W. Liming, Becci Akin, and Jody Brook, "Adverse Childhood Experiences and Foster Care Placement Stability," *Pediatrics* 148, no. 6 (2021): e2021052700. Liming et al. used an expanded adversity inventory; counts are not directly comparable to the ten-item ACE questionnaire used elsewhere in this book. See also Kristin Turney and Christopher Wildeman, "Adverse Childhood Experiences Among Children Placed in and Adopted from Foster Care: Evidence from a Nationally Representative Survey," *Child Abuse & Neglect* 64 (2017): 117–129.

PART FOUR

FROM DIAGNOSIS TO PRESCRIPTION

CHAPTER TWELVE

Start Where You Are

> "Do not despise these small beginnings, for the Lord rejoices to see the work begin."
>
> –Zechariah 4:10 (NLT)

WE HAVE SPENT THE first three parts of this book seeing the wound clearly.

We have seen the neurobiological damage that childhood trauma inflicts—how it rewires developing brains, dysregulates nervous systems, and creates injuries that persist for decades. We have seen the church's blindness—how it mistakes symptoms for sins, how it offers spiritual solutions to medical problems, how its theology sometimes compounds the very wounds it seeks to heal. We have seen the hemorrhage—the exodus of the wounded, the addiction crisis, the families caught in cycles they do not understand, the pastors breaking under weights they were never trained to carry.

If I have done my job, you now see what you could not see before. You understand why the church is bleeding. You understand what is at stake.

Now what?

Part Four is about transformation. About moving from diagnosis to treatment. From understanding the problem to becoming the solution. From being a church that unknowingly wounds to a church that intentionally heals.

But before I lay out a comprehensive framework for that transformation—and I will, in the next chapter—I want to start with something simpler.

I want to tell you what you can do this week.

The Monday Morning Question

If you have read this far, you already know more about childhood trauma than most pastors in America. That is not a criticism of those pastors. It is the reality of a crisis that the church has only begun to recognize. You are ahead of the curve simply by reading this book.

And that means you can start making a difference right now. Not next year. Not after you have built a program or hired a counselor or restructured your entire ministry. Today.

The simplest, most powerful thing you can do is change one question.

Stop asking "What is wrong with you?" and start asking "What happened to you?"

That single shift—from judgment to curiosity, from diagnosis to discovery—changes everything. It changes how you hear the man who cannot control his anger. It changes how you respond to the woman whose anxiety makes her miss church for weeks at a time. It changes how you counsel the couple whose marriage is disintegrating in ways that make no sense until you understand their childhoods.

You do not need a certification to ask a better question. You do not need a budget. You just need the willingness to stop assuming you know what is wrong and start wondering what happened.

"What happened to you?" is a better question than "What is wrong with you?" but it is still a question, and questions open doors. Before you walk through one, know four things.

You are not asking for a story. You are offering a door. Do not press. "I have noticed you seem to be carrying something. If you ever want to talk about it, I am here," leaves the choice with them. That choice is the whole point. Trauma is what happens when someone's choices are taken away. Do not take them again in the name of helping.

Know what you cannot promise. In most states, clergy are mandated reporters when a child is at risk. Find out what your state requires before you are sitting across from someone, not after. And say it out loud at the start, "If you tell me a child is being hurt, I am required to report it. Everything else stays with me." People can handle a limit. They cannot handle a betrayal.

Know where the door leads. Do not open a wound you have nowhere to send. Before you ask the question, build the list—two or three trauma-trained therapists in your area, what they charge, whether they take insurance, and how a person actually gets an appointment. A referral is not passing someone off. It is the difference between a pastor and a surgeon, and both are needed.

Know what you are. You are not the treatment. You are the one who sees the wound, names it out loud, and stays with the person while someone trained sets the bone. That is not the smaller job. In this book it is the whole job.

Ask the question and be prepared for what you are opening.
That is where transformation begins.

What to Read

The science behind what you have learned in this book did not emerge in a vacuum. Researchers and clinicians have been documenting the impact of childhood trauma for decades. If you want to go deeper—and you should—here is where to start.

- *The Body Keeps the Score* by Dr. Bessel van der Kolk. This is the book that brought trauma science to the mainstream. Van der Kolk spent decades researching how trauma lives in the body, not just the mind, and why traditional talk therapy often is not enough. If you read only one book beyond this one, make it this. You will never look at a struggling congregant the same way again.

- *The Deepest Well* by Dr. Nadine Burke Harris. Burke Harris was a pediatrician in one of San Francisco's poorest neighborhoods when she discovered the ACE Study and realized that the children she was treating were not sick because of bad luck or bad genetics—they were sick because of what had happened to them. This book makes the science personal and urgent. It will break your heart and give you hope in the same 300 pages.

- *The Adverse Childhood Experiences Recovery Workbook* by Dr. Glenn Schiraldi. Where other books explain the problem,

Schiraldi provides a practical path to healing. His workbook gives trauma survivors concrete tools for recovery, grounded in both clinical evidence and compassion. Schiraldi's 14 books on trauma recovery and resilience represent some of the most accessible clinical resources available. He is also a person of faith who understands the intersection of trauma, addiction, and spiritual formation—and as you will learn in the next chapter, he serves as Dean of UACT Academy and chairs our Mental Health Advisory Board.

- The ACE Study itself. The original 1998 study by Felitti and Anda is available online. Read it. It is not long. Understanding the data that changed everything—that childhood trauma predicts heart disease, cancer, suicide, addiction, and nearly every major cause of death—will give you the foundation to explain this crisis to your leadership team, your elders, your congregation. When someone asks why this matters, you will have the numbers.

These books will not make you a trauma therapist. They should not. That is not your role. But they will give you the knowledge base to understand what your people are carrying and why your current approach may not be reaching them.

What to Learn

Beyond reading, there are frameworks and resources that can begin shifting how your church thinks about trauma.

SAMHSA's Trauma-Informed Care Framework. The Substance Abuse and Mental Health Services Administration—a federal agency—has published comprehensive guidelines for organizations seeking to become trauma-informed. Their six principles of trauma-informed care—safety, trustworthiness and transparency, peer support, collaboration and mutuality, empowerment and choice, and cultural sensitivity—provide a starting vocabulary for any organization. These resources are free and publicly available. They are a good place to begin. They are not, as you will see, a destination.

ACE screening and scoring. Learn how to explain ACE scores to your staff and volunteers. You do not need to formally screen your congregation, and in most cases you should not without proper training and support systems in place. But understanding what an ACE score is, what the research says about the cumulative impact of multiple adverse experiences, and how prevalent high ACE scores are in any given population—that changes how you plan ministry. When you understand that more than half your congregation carries at least one ACE, and that one in five may carry four or more, you stop designing ministry for the healthy and start designing it for the wounded.

Local mental health partnerships. This week, find out who the trauma-specialized therapists are in your area. Not just any counselor—specifically those trained in EMDR, Somatic Experiencing, or other evidence-based trauma therapies. Build a referral list. When someone comes to you in crisis, you need to know where to send them—not next month after you have done the research, but that afternoon. A pastor with a referral list is exponentially more helpful than a pastor with good intentions and no names.

What to Change This Week

Beyond reading and learning, there are practical shifts you can begin making immediately in how your church operates. None of these require a budget. All of them require intention.

- **Audit your language from the pulpit.** Listen to your own sermons with new ears. How often do you use phrases like "just trust God," "let go and let God," "if you had enough faith," "there must be unconfessed sin"? These phrases, offered with genuine pastoral care, can land on traumatized nervous systems like accusations. You do not have to stop preaching truth. You have to start delivering it in ways that wounded people can actually receive. That means acknowledging suffering without rushing to fix it. It means saying, "this is hard and God is still here" instead of "if you just believed more, this would go away."

- **Brief your staff and key volunteers.** You do not need a formal training program to have a conversation. Share what you have learned. Explain the ACE Study. Talk about the difference between spiritual struggles and neurobiological injuries. Give your team permission to say "I do not know how to help you with this, but I know someone who can"—and make sure they actually have a name to offer.

- **Create one safe space.** Identify one environment in your church—a small group, a ministry team, a pastoral conversation—where people can be honest about what they are carrying without being met with platitudes or prescriptions. This does not require a new program. It requires a culture shift in one room. Start small. Let people bleed without trying to stop the bleeding with Bible verses.

- **Stop rewarding the fawn response.** Remember the Four F's from earlier in this book. The person who never says no, who serves until they collapse, who abandons their own needs to keep everyone happy—you may be holding them up as a model of Christian service. They may actually be running a trauma survival program. Pay attention. Ask how they are really doing. Give them permission to rest without feeling like they are failing God.

Who Is Already Moving

You are not the first pastor to feel this urgency. Across the country, there are early signs that the church is beginning to wake up.

Some seminaries have started integrating trauma awareness into their pastoral training programs. Organizations like the Faith-Based Trauma-Informed Care Alliance are developing toolkits for congregations. Theologians like Shelly Rambo at Boston University and Serene Jones at Union Theological Seminary have begun the academic work of integrating trauma research with Christian theology. Individual churches—scattered, unconnected, often working in isolation—have started training their pastoral care teams in basic trauma awareness.

These are encouraging signs. I do not want to minimize them.

But I do want to be honest about their limitations.

Most of what exists today is scattered. A workshop here. A toolkit there. A seminary course that covers trauma in a single lecture within a broader counseling class. A church that sends its pastor to a daylong training and then goes back to business as usual. These efforts are well-intentioned, and they matter. But they are not systematic. They do not transform organizations. They do not close the gap between knowing about trauma and actually doing something about it.

A pastor who reads *The Body Keeps the Score* and understands ACEs is better equipped than one who does not. But understanding alone does not change how a church operates. It does not restructure children's ministry. It does not retrain the prayer team. It does not create protocols for crisis response. It does not build the partnerships with clinical professionals that wounded people desperately need. It does not measure whether anyone is actually healing.

Knowledge is the starting line. It is not the finish.

Reading books gets you to awareness. What gets you from awareness to transformation?

That requires a framework—a clear map showing where you are, where you need to go, and what it takes to get there. A way to measure your progress honestly, not just your intentions.

That is what the next chapter provides.

The Honest Starting Point

Let me say something that may sound strange coming from the author of a book about this crisis.

I am not asking you to be perfect at this.

I am asking you to start.

The difference between a church that is helping its wounded people and a church that is failing them is not expertise. It is willingness. Willingness to see what you have not seen. Willingness to admit that your current approach is not reaching everyone. Willingness to learn what you do not know and build what does not yet exist.

You will make mistakes. You will say the wrong thing to a trauma survivor. You will underestimate the depth of someone's wound. You will overestimate your ability to help. That is okay. The wounded people in your congregation have survived far worse than your imperfect attempts to care for them.

What they cannot survive is your refusal to try.

So start where you are. Read the books. Learn the science. Change the questions. Build the referral list. Create one safe space. Brief your team. And then—when you are ready to go further, when awareness is no longer enough and you want your entire church to become a place where wounded people actually heal—turn the page.

The framework for that transformation is waiting.

CHAPTER THIRTEEN

From Blind to Seeing

A New Framework

> "The beginning of wisdom is this: Get wisdom. Though it cost all you have, get understanding."
>
> –Proverbs 4:7

THE PREVIOUS CHAPTER GAVE you a place to start. Books to read. Questions to change. Practical steps you can take this week to begin seeing what you have been missing.

But starting is not the same as arriving.

A pastor who understands ACEs is better than one who does not. A church that has a referral list of trauma-informed therapists is better than one that sends struggling people home with a prayer. Awareness matters. First steps matter.

And they are not enough.

The crisis documented in this book—1,401 Americans dying every day from the downstream effects of childhood trauma, 70% of your congregation carrying wounds the church has been misdiagnosing for 2,000 years—will not be solved by awareness alone. It requires transformation. And transformation requires more than good intentions. It requires a framework. A clear understanding of where you are, where you need to go, and what it takes to get there.

This chapter introduces that framework.

The Problem with "Trauma-Informed"

Walk into almost any church today that has done any work on mental health, and you will hear them describe themselves as "trauma-informed."

The pastor attended a workshop. The youth ministry added a training module. Someone on staff read a book about ACEs. And now they have checked the box. Trauma-informed. Done.

Except nothing has actually changed.

The term "trauma-informed" has become so diluted that it no longer means anything. It has become a buzzword—a credential to claim without any measurable standard behind it. When everyone is trauma-informed, no one is trauma-informed.

This is not just annoying. It is dangerous. It gives churches permission to believe they have addressed the problem when they have merely acknowledged it exists. It creates a false sense of competency that leaves wounded people just as vulnerable as before—sometimes more so, because now they expect help and find only jargon.

The resources I recommended in the last chapter—the books, the SAMHSA framework, the local partnerships—are essential starting points. They will help you understand the problem. They will begin shifting your language and your awareness. On the four-level scale I am about to describe, they will move you from Level 1 to Level 2, but there is a ceiling.

We need a framework that distinguishes between organizations that know about trauma and organizations that actually do something about it. One that creates clear standards rather than vague claims. One that closes the gap between knowing and doing.

The Four Levels of Trauma Response

Through years of research, corporate consulting, and working with faith communities, I have developed a classification system that distinguishes between four distinct levels of trauma response. This is not academic theory. This is a practical framework based on what differentiates organizations that are failing the wounded from organizations that are healing them.

Level 1: Trauma-Unaware

"We do not have a trauma problem here."

Organizations at this level either deny the existence of trauma or actively ignore its impact. They operate under the assumption that people's problems stem primarily from personal failures, poor choices, or—in church contexts—sin and weak faith.

In churches, Level 1 looks like this: depression means you are not praying enough. Anxiety is evidence of insufficient faith. If you needed therapy, you would not really trust God. Behavioral issues in children are spiritual rebellion requiring discipline. Addiction is a moral failure demanding repentance.

The language reveals the mindset: "They just need more discipline." "People need to take personal responsibility." "We cannot coddle everyone."

These are not necessarily bad people. They are operating from a worldview that predates our understanding of trauma's neurobiological impact. They genuinely believe they are helping. But Level 1 organizations actively harm the wounded—retraumatizing them through harsh responses, driving them into hiding, and confirming their worst fears that they are fundamentally defective.

Level 2: Trauma-Aware

"Trauma exists, but we are not sure what to do."

Organizations at this level recognize that trauma is real and affects people, but they lack systematic approaches to address it. They have good intentions and may have provided some basic education, but their responses remain inconsistent and reactive.

In churches, Level 2 looks like this: the pastor occasionally mentions mental health from the pulpit. Some people are in therapy—quietly. There is a vague acknowledgment that "people are struggling." When crises happen, the response is well-meaning but improvised. "Here is a therapist's number" is the extent of support. Leaders care deeply but feel overwhelmed and inadequate.

This is where most churches land after reading books, attending workshops, or implementing the steps from the previous chapter. And it represents real progress. But Level 2 churches are like doctors who can diagnose pneumonia but do not know antibiotics exist. They can see the problem. They care about the problem. Their tools are inadequate for the problem.

The result: less stigma than Level 1, but most wounded people are still suffering. The approach is crisis-driven rather than proactive, reactive rather than systemic. Good hearts, limited impact. People still leaving, just slower.

Level 3: Trauma-Informed

"We understand and have systematic responses."

This is where most organizations aspire to be, and it represents significant achievement. Level 3 organizations have implemented comprehensive policies, provided systematic training, and modified their environments to prevent re-traumatization. They operate from established principles: safety, trustworthiness, peer support, collaboration, empowerment, and cultural sensitivity.

In churches, Level 3 looks like this: leadership has been trained in ACEs and neuroscience. Trauma-sensitive language is used consistently—"What happened to you?" instead of "What is wrong with you?" Policies protect vulnerable people. Referral networks with trauma-specialized therapists exist. Mental health is openly discussed without stigma.

This is good. This matters. This is infinitely better than Level 1 or 2.

But here is the critical distinction: trauma-informed organizations focus primarily on avoiding harm rather than actively promoting healing.

They create safe spaces. They respond empathetically. They do not retraumatize. But they do not necessarily provide interventions that help people actually heal from trauma's effects. They accommodate the wound without treating it.

Level 3 organizations know about trauma, but that knowledge has not yet transformed into systematic action that produces measurable healing.

Level 4: Trauma-Responsive

"We do not just understand—we actively heal and prevent."

This is the destination. Level 4 organizations go beyond preventing re-traumatization to actively promoting healing and post-traumatic growth. They provide trauma-specific interventions, measure healing outcomes, and integrate recovery into their core mission.

In churches, Level 4 looks like this: every staff member and volunteer is trauma-trained and certified. Financial support for members' therapy is available. Professional partnerships are strong and formalized. Trauma-responsiveness shapes every aspect of ministry—worship, preaching, children's ministry, youth programs, small groups, counseling, community outreach. Healing outcomes are actually measured. Preventive ministry exists: parenting classes, foster parent training and support, marriage enrichment with trauma awareness. The community knows this church as a place where wounded people find real help.

At Level 4, trauma-responsiveness is not a program. It is an identity. The church has become what it was always meant to be: a sanctuary. Not just a building where people gather, but a place of genuine safety and refuge where the brokenhearted are actually bound up and the captives are actually set free.

Level 4 churches do not just talk about healing. They produce it.

The Critical Distinction

Let me make this as clear as possible.

Trauma-informed means knowing about trauma's impact.
Trauma-responsive means knowing and doing something effective about it.

A trauma-informed church knows that 70% of its congregation carries childhood trauma.
A trauma-responsive church has restructured everything around that reality.

A trauma-informed church can explain what ACEs are.
A trauma-responsive church measures its members' healing outcomes.

A trauma-informed church has read books about trauma.
A trauma-responsive church has every leader trained and certified in trauma-responsive ministry.

And most churches that claim to be trauma-informed are actually trauma-aware at best—they know the vocabulary without having done the work. They have checked the awareness box without transforming their practice.

The goal of this book is to help you close that gap. To move from knowing to doing. From informed to responsive. From accommodation to transformation.

Where Is Your Church?

Be honest with yourself. Where does your church currently operate?

If your leaders have never been trained in trauma, if your counseling approach is purely spiritual, if you have never heard the term "ACE score" in a staff meeting—you are at Level 1. There is no shame in this. It is where almost everyone starts. But you cannot stay there.

If you have some awareness but nothing has actually changed in how you operate—you are at Level 2. You have the vocabulary but not the practice. You are aware but not equipped.

If you have begun making changes—training leaders, adjusting practices, building referral networks—but trauma-responsiveness is still a program rather than an identity, you are at Level 3. You are on the right path. Keep going.

If trauma-responsiveness shapes everything you do, if every leader is trained and certified, if your community knows you as a place where wounded people find real help—you are at Level 4. You are rare. And you are what the church needs to become.

Most churches reading this book are at Level 1 or Level 2. That is not a criticism. It is simply reality. The question is not where you are. The question is whether you are willing to move.

Why I Built UACT

I need to be transparent with you about something.

When I began researching childhood trauma—first for a memoir about my own family, then with growing alarm as I discovered the scale of the crisis—I assumed someone had already built a solution for the church. I assumed that somewhere out there, an organization had developed a comprehensive framework for transforming faith communities from trauma-unaware to trauma-responsive. A training curriculum. An assessment tool. A certification program. A systematic approach to closing the knowing-doing gap.

I searched. For months, I searched. I found wonderful individual efforts—a workshop here, a toolkit there, a seminary course, a brave pastor doing what they could with limited resources. But I could not find anyone who had built a comprehensive system specifically designed to move churches from Level 1 through Level 4. Nothing that addressed theology and neuroscience together. Nothing that trained entire organizations rather than individual leaders. Nothing that measured outcomes rather than intentions.

So I built one.

United Against Childhood Trauma (UACT) is the nonprofit organization I founded to address this crisis. I am telling you this not as a sales pitch but as an honest disclosure, because Allison, my editor, rightly told me that readers deserve to know where the framework in this book comes from and who is behind it.

UACT exists to pursue what some might call an audacious goal: ending the cycle of childhood trauma through three pillars—Awareness, Healing Interventions, and Prevention. I know that sounds enormous. It is enormous. But I spent decades in the corporate world solving problems that seemed impossible until someone built a system to solve them. I have 14 patents. I have advised NASA and the United Nations. I have built enterprise software platforms that serve Fortune 100 companies. I know what it takes to build systems that work at scale.

And I know that to solve a giant problem, you need a giant goal.

The difference between UACT and wishful thinking is rigor. It is the people I have assembled, the tools we have developed, and the framework we are building—not from theory alone, but from the intersection of clinical expertise, research evidence, corporate systems thinking, and deep Christian faith.

Let me introduce you to the team behind the tools.

The People Behind the Framework

UACT's Mental Health Advisory Board is comprised of mental health professionals who are also people of faith—practitioners who understand both the neuroscience of trauma and the particular needs of faith communities.

Dr. Glenn Schiraldi, PhD, LTC (USAR, Ret.) serves as Dean of UACT Academy and chairs the Advisory Board. Schiraldi is the founder and CEO of Resilience Training International and the author of 14 books on trauma recovery and resilience. His work has focused specifically on the intersection of faith, addiction, and trauma—the exact convergence that this book addresses. His Adverse Childhood Experiences Recovery Workbook is one of the most widely used clinical tools in trauma recovery.

Dr. Lee Long, President and CEO of Restoration Counseling and President of the International Cognitive Behavioral Analysis System of Psychotherapy (CBASP) Society, brings decades of clinical experience in evidence-based therapeutic approaches for chronic depression and interpersonal trauma—the conditions most commonly found in faith communities dealing with unaddressed childhood adversity.

Kristin Trudeau, LPC-MHSP, LADAC II, CFRC—therapist, Licensed Addictions Counselor, and Certified First Responder Counselor—brings frontline clinical experience with the populations churches encounter most often: people struggling with addiction, first responders carrying occupational trauma, and families in crisis.

Deborah McNelis, M.Ed., author of The First 60 Days, creator of the Neuro-Nurturing® Model, and founder of Brain Insights, LLC, brings expertise in early childhood brain development—the developmental window where trauma does its most profound damage, and where prevention can have its greatest impact.

These are not armchair theorists. They are practitioners who directly support trauma survivors, researchers who study what works, and people of faith who understand why the church matters in this equation. The assessment tool I am about to describe was developed under their guidance, built on their collective expertise, and grounded in the established evidence base for trauma-informed organizational transformation.

The Faith Community Trauma-Responsive Index

The Faith Community Trauma-Responsive Index (FCTI) is a comprehensive 150-point assessment tool designed specifically for faith communities. To our knowledge, it is the only tool of its kind: an instrument that measures a church's actual capacity to recognize, respond to, and facilitate healing from childhood trauma across every dimension of congregational life.

The FCTI was built on the foundation of SAMHSA's validated framework for trauma-informed care, adapted and expanded for the specific context of faith communities. It was developed by UACT's Mental Health Advisory Board in 2025.

I want to be honest with you: The FCTI is a new tool. It has not been through decades of independent validation studies. As of this writing, we are preparing pilot programs with churches who want to be among the first to undergo rigorous assessment. By the time you read this, those pilots may be underway or completed.

I tell you this not to undermine the tool's credibility but to establish it. I would rather be honest about where we are than pretend we have a 30-year track record we do not. What we do have is a team of credentialed professionals who built this assessment on established research, validated frameworks, and decades of combined clinical experience. What we have is a tool that no one else has built, because no one else has tried.

We also have a conviction that honest assessment—even imperfect assessment—is infinitely better than no assessment at all.

Let me walk you through what the FCTI measures. Not to enable you to do it yourself—the assessment requires trained evaluators for reasons I will explain—but so you understand the scope of what genuine trauma-responsiveness requires.

The Six Domains

The FCTI evaluates churches across six domains, drawn from SAMHSA's established principles and expanded for faith community contexts:

Domain 1: Leadership Awareness and Theological Integration (25 points). This domain assesses whether senior leaders actually understand childhood trauma. Not just the vocabulary, but the neuroscience, the prevalence data, and the intersection with spiritual formation. It evaluates whether the church has developed a coherent theology that integrates trauma awareness with biblical truth—the kind of theological reframing we explored in Part Two. And it examines whether trauma-responsiveness is a strategic priority with real resources behind it, or just another initiative that gets lip service.

Domain 2: Congregational Training and Capacity Building (25 points). This domain measures training depth and breadth. Have pastors and elders completed advanced trauma-responsive ministry certification—not a two-hour workshop, but substantive training? Are ministry staff and volunteers trained? Is the entire congregation being educated, or just leadership? The difference between Level 3 and Level 4 often shows up here—in whether training is superficial or substantive, optional or required, one-time or ongoing.

Domain 3: Environment, Culture, and Safety (30 points). This is the largest domain because environment shapes everything. It assesses the physical space. Are there quiet rooms for those who become overwhelmed? Is worship predictable enough that trauma survivors can feel safe? It examines relational culture. Are there healthy power dynamics or authoritarian patterns that trigger trauma survivors? Is the spiritual atmosphere grace-centered or shame-driven? Can wounded people bleed in the pews without judgment?

Domain 4: Support Systems and Healing Resources (30 points). This domain evaluates the actual infrastructure for healing. Is pastoral care trauma-informed? Does the church have vetted referral relationships with trauma-specialized therapists? Are there financial resources to help members access professional treatment? Does peer support exist—trained lay counselors, support groups, small group leaders who understand trauma? Is there a first-responder system for crisis moments?

Domain 5: Ministry Programming and Implementation (25 points). This domain examines how trauma-responsiveness shows up in actual ministry. Is preaching designed with trauma survivors in mind—acknowledging real suffering without platitudes or victim-blaming theology? Is children's and youth ministry trauma-informed, recognizing that many young people are experiencing trauma in real time? Does the church extend its trauma-responsive ministry into the community, or does healing stop at the church doors?

Domain 6: Measurement, Accountability, and Continuous Improvement (15 points). This final domain asks the question that separates serious organizations from those playing at transformation. Do you measure outcomes? Do you track whether wounded people are actually healing, or do you assume effectiveness without evidence? Do you seek feedback from trauma survivors about what is working and what is causing harm? Do you pursue external assessment to ensure objectivity?

What the Assessment Reveals

Each domain contains detailed assessment criteria, specific scoring guidelines, and clear thresholds that distinguish between levels. The total 150-point scale maps directly to the four levels:

1. 0–37 points: Level 1 (Trauma-Unaware)
2. 38–75 points: Level 2 (Trauma-Aware)
3. 76–113 points: Level 3 (Trauma-Informed)
4. 114–150 points: Level 4 (Trauma-Responsive)

Here is where the practical steps from the previous chapter fit in. Reading the recommended books, learning about ACEs, changing your language, building a referral list—these actions alone might move a church from the 10 to 20-point range into the high 30s or low 40s. Real progress. A meaningful shift from Unaware to Aware.

But to cross into Level 3—genuine, systematic trauma-informed practice—requires organizational change: comprehensive training, environmental modifications, formalized partnerships, and theological integration. And to reach Level 4—where the church is actively producing healing, measuring outcomes, and preventing trauma—requires the kind of sustained, expert-guided transformation that no book or workshop can deliver alone.

The assessment does more than assign a score. It identifies specific strengths to build on and gaps to address. It creates a roadmap—showing exactly what needs to change to move from one level to the next. And it establishes a baseline against which future progress can be measured.

When Leadership Is Divided

I want to address something that happens in nearly every church that confronts this issue: not everyone in leadership will agree that this matters.

Some will feel the urgency immediately. They will read this book and recognize the faces in their congregation. They will connect the struggling marriages, the addictions, the departures, the anxiety they see every Sunday to the crisis described in these pages.

Others will resist. Not because they do not care, but because the implications are overwhelming. Becoming trauma-responsive means rethinking how you preach, how you counsel, how you train volunteers, how you structure small groups, how you spend money. It means admitting that some of what you have been doing—with the best of intentions—has not been working. That is a hard thing to admit.

If your leadership team is divided, here is what I recommend.

Do not wait for unanimous agreement. You will not get it. Start with the willing. Find the two or three leaders who feel what you feel, who see what you see, and begin with them. Read this book together. Discuss it. Let the weight of the evidence do its work.

Then take a small, measurable step. Pick one ministry—children's ministry, pastoral counseling, small groups—and pilot a trauma-responsive approach. Document what changes. Let results speak louder than arguments.

Meanwhile, invite the skeptics to engage, not with pressure but with curiosity. Ask them: "What would change your mind?" Give them the data. Give them the stories. Give them time. Some leaders need to see it work before they believe it can.

And if some leaders never come around—if they remain convinced that the church's only job is spiritual formation and that trauma is someone else's problem—you may need to lead without them. The wounded people in your congregation cannot wait for a unanimous vote. They are bleeding now.

A Word About Self-Assessment

I have deliberately avoided providing enough detail for you to score your own church on the FCTI. This is not about protecting proprietary information. It is about protecting you and the people you serve.

Self-assessment in this arena is dangerous. The domains I described sound straightforward, but the actual criteria require expertise to apply correctly. A church can convince itself it scores high on "grace-centered spiritual culture" while trauma survivors in that same church experience it as deeply shame-based. Leaders can believe they have created safe environments while remaining blind to power dynamics that re-traumatize.

The point of assessment is not to assign a number. It is to identify a path forward. That path requires outside perspective—not because churches lack intelligence, but because they lack objectivity about themselves. An outside assessment brings perspective that insiders cannot provide, no matter how well-intentioned.

I have seen it in the corporate world for 30 years. The organizations most convinced they do not need outside evaluation are the ones that need it most. Churches are no different.

The Stakes

Let me remind you what is at stake.

Every day, approximately 1,401 Americans die from health conditions attributable to childhood trauma—heart disease, cancer, diabetes, suicide, overdose. Many of them sat in church pews. Many of them came looking for help and found only spiritual band-aids for neurobiological wounds. Many of them left believing they were beyond help, that their faith was insufficient, that God had abandoned them.

This hemorrhage will not stop because we mean well or pray sincerely or believe ourselves to be compassionate. It will only stop when churches transform from organizations that unknowingly wound into organizations that intentionally heal.

That transformation requires knowing where you actually are—not where you hope you are or believe you are, but where you actually are. It requires a framework that distinguishes between talking about trauma and doing something about it. It requires honest assessment, professional guidance, and sustained commitment.

The four levels give you the map. The six domains show you the terrain. The assessment gives you your location. What remains is the willingness to make the journey.

The Road Ahead

In the remaining chapters, we will walk that road together. You will hear my own story—how I came to this work, what I learned growing up as one of 14 children in a household shaped by trauma, and why I left a successful corporate career to sound the alarm on this crisis. You will learn practical steps for moving your church from one level to the next. And you will see a vision for what becomes possible when the church finally becomes what it was always meant to be.

The church was always meant to be a hospital for the sick, not a museum for the saints.

It is time to become what we were called to be.

CHAPTER FOURTEEN

The Mirror and the Window

"Physician, heal yourself."

–Luke 4:23

IN THE LAST CHAPTER, I walked you through a framework for assessing where your church stands on its journey toward becoming trauma-responsive. The four levels. The six domains. The 150-point assessment tool that measures organizational capacity. What I was really describing was how a church looks into its own mirror—an honest, unflinching look at what is actually there. Not what you hope to see. Not what your mission statement says. What is actually there.

But organizational transformation is not enough.

Churches do not heal people. God heals people. And God uses people to heal people. And the people who lead your church—pastors, elders, staff, volunteers—cannot lead others to healing places they have never visited themselves.

This chapter is about the mirror that comes before the organizational mirror. The personal mirror. The one that requires each leader—each person who wants to help—to look at their own story before they attempt to help others with theirs.

And I want to be clear: what I'm about to describe is not just for pastors. It's for anyone who wants to walk alongside a wounded person. Sunday school teachers. Small group leaders. Deacons. Foster parents. Counselors. Parents who suspect their child is carrying something heavy. If you want to help someone else heal, this chapter is for you.

The principle is simple. The practice is hard.

First the Mirror. Then the Window.

The Mirror is about looking inward—at your own childhood, your own family history, your own experiences, your own wounds. It requires brutal honesty about what happened to you and how it has shaped who you have become.

The Window is about looking outward—at others, at your congregation, at the wounded people you are called to serve. It is about seeing their pain clearly and responding with wisdom and skill.

The sequence is not optional. The Mirror must come before the Window.

You cannot truly see the wounds in others until you have acknowledged the wounds in yourself. You cannot lead people to healing places you have not been willing to visit. You cannot offer what you do not possess.

Think of it like the safety announcement on every commercial flight: In the unlikely event of a loss of cabin pressure, oxygen masks will drop from the panel above. Please secure your own mask before assisting others.

The instruction seems counterintuitive. Shouldn't we help the vulnerable first? But the wisdom is profound. If you pass out from oxygen deprivation while trying to help someone else, you have helped no one. You must be breathing before you can help others breathe.

The same principle applies here.

If you are among the 70%—and statistically, most readers of this book will be—you cannot effectively walk alongside wounded people while your own trauma remains unexamined. You will have blind spots you cannot see. You will be triggered by situations you do not understand. You will unconsciously avoid topics that touch your own unhealed places. You will bleed on the people you are supposed to serve.

The work starts with you.

Why the Mirror Comes First

In Chapter 3, we talked about what trauma does to the brain. The amygdala gets stuck in threat-detection mode. The prefrontal cortex—the part that reasons, plans, and regulates emotion—gets overridden. The hippocampus, which processes memory, gets disrupted so that past events feel like present dangers. The nervous system stays locked in fight, flight, fawn, or freeze long after the original threat is gone.

This happens to everyone. Including leaders. Including you.

And here is why that matters for anyone trying to help wounded people: You cannot create safety if your own nervous system is dysregulated. Trauma survivors are hypervigilant. They read body language, tone, and micro expressions with uncanny accuracy—because their survival once depended on it. If your nervous system is running hot underneath your calm exterior, they will sense it. They will not feel safe with you no matter what words you say. You cannot fake safety. You can only embody it. And you can only embody it if you have done your own work.

You cannot see clearly through a dirty window. Unexamined trauma distorts perception. You will misread situations through the lens of your own wounds. You will be triggered by people and topics that touch your unhealed places, and your reactions will confuse and harm those you are trying to help. Remember what we learned about the amygdala—it does not distinguish between a real threat and a reminder of an old one. If your amygdala is still reacting to wounds from 30 years ago, it will hijack your responses to the person sitting across from you right now.

You cannot teach what you do not know. If you have never walked the path of healing, you cannot guide others on it. You will give advice that sounds good but does not work. You will offer platitudes instead of pathways. You will promise hope without providing tools.

You cannot sustain this work from a place of personal unhealth. Walking alongside wounded people is exhausting. If you are doing it while carrying your own unprocessed pain, you will burn out. You will become resentful. You will sabotage the very work you are trying to do—not intentionally, but inevitably.

None of this is disqualifying. If we disqualified everyone with trauma from helping others, we would have no helpers. The 70% prevalence means most people in ministry have experienced childhood adversity. The question is not whether you have wounds. The question is whether you have done the work to heal—or whether you are bleeding on the people you are supposed to serve.

Pastor Andrew

Let me tell you about a pastor I'll call Andrew.

Andrew was a successful senior pastor of a growing church. He preached powerfully. He led confidently. He was respected in his denomination and his community. From the outside, he looked like someone who had it all together.

What no one knew: Andrew grew up with a father who was emotionally absent and a mother who was chronically depressed. He learned early on that no one was coming to rescue him—that if he wanted anything in life, he would have to earn it through relentless effort. He became a high achiever. He excelled in school, in sports, in ministry. He never stopped moving because stopping meant feeling, and feeling meant pain.

Think about that through the lens of Chapter 3. Andrew's nervous system quickly learned that rest was dangerous. His amygdala associated stillness with the pain of an empty household. So he stayed in perpetual flight mode—not running from a predator but running from his own interior life. His workaholism was not ambition. It was a trauma response that looked like dedication.

His trauma expressed itself in ministry as perfectionism and control. He worked eighty-hour weeks. He could not delegate because no one met his standards. He micromanaged his staff into frustration and turnover. He preached grace but modeled performance.

His church grew numerically while his staff grew resentful and his family grew distant.

Andrew had never looked in the Mirror. He did not even know there was a mirror to look into.

What the Mirror Looks Like

What does it mean to look into the Mirror? It starts with a simple question: What happened to me?

Take the ACE questionnaire[1] if you have not already. Be honest with yourself about what you experienced in childhood. Count the categories—not to label yourself, but to understand yourself. Your score is not your destiny. But it is information you need.

Then go deeper. Consider whether patterns in your life might trace back to early experiences.

Do you struggle with workaholism? That might be a trauma response—proving your worth through performance because you never felt inherently valuable as a child. Do you avoid conflict at all costs? That might be a trauma response—keeping the peace because conflict in your childhood meant danger. Do you need constant approval? That might be a trauma response—seeking external validation because you never received unconditional love. Do you have difficulty trusting others? That might be a trauma response—your nervous system learned early on that people cannot be relied upon. Do you rage when criticized? That might be a trauma response—your amygdala experiencing any critique as the rejection you feared as a child. Do you feel like an imposter despite your accomplishments? That might be a trauma response—the shame you absorbed early in life telling you that you do not deserve success.

These are not weaknesses to be ashamed of. They are adaptations that once helped you survive. Your brain did exactly what it was designed to do—it protected you. But those survival strategies may be limiting your effectiveness now. And they are certainly affecting how you relate to wounded people.

Andrew recognized himself in that list. Workaholism. Perfectionism. Inability to delegate. The need to control every outcome. When he first encountered the Mirror concept during a leadership training, something cracked open.

He realized, for the first time in his 52 years, that his relentless drive was not ambition. It was survival. His inability to rest was not dedication. It was fear. His perfectionism was not excellence. It was the terrified child inside him trying to earn the love he never received.

Andrew wept in that training session. Not because he was weak, but because he finally saw himself clearly.

Getting Help

Looking in the Mirror is the first step. But seeing is not healing.

Andrew entered therapy—something he had privately scorned for years as unnecessary for someone with genuine faith. He discovered that his ACE score was higher than he had realized, because he had normalized experiences that were actually traumatic. He began the slow, painful, beautiful work of healing.

Here is what I am asking of anyone who recognizes themselves in this chapter.

Find a therapist who specializes in trauma. Not a general counselor, but someone specifically trained in trauma treatment. Ask about their experience with evidence-based approaches like EMDR[2], somatic therapies, or Internal Family Systems. A good trauma therapist can help you process what happened in ways that talk therapy alone often cannot.

I have seen this firsthand. My own brother Jamie prayed for 30 years for relief from depression. Seven sessions of EMDR produced more healing than three decades of prayer alone. He was not healed by abandoning faith. He was healed by adding competent treatment to his faith. God heals through many means. Sometimes the answer to prayer is a skilled professional who knows how to help your nervous system find peace.

Keep working. Healing is not a one-time event. It is an ongoing process. Stay in therapy as long as you need to. Build relationships that support your healing. Do the work.

If cost is a barrier, look for options. Many therapists offer sliding-scale fees. Some churches have benevolence funds that can cover mental health care. Community mental health centers offer reduced rates. The investment is worth it—not just for your own wellbeing, but for the wellbeing of everyone you serve.

Healing Is Not Weakness

I know what some of you are thinking. I am a leader. I cannot show weakness. If my congregation knew I was in therapy, they would lose confidence in me. A pastor is supposed to have it together. I am supposed to be the one helping others, not the one needing help.

This is exactly the thinking that perpetuates the crisis.

Seeking healing is not weakness. It is wisdom. It is recognition that you cannot pour from an empty cup. It is humility—the acknowledgment that you are not above the human condition, not exempt from the effects of your own history.

I am not asking you to expose all your wounds to your congregation. Appropriate boundaries are essential. Your healing is your business. You do not need to share your ACE score from the pulpit.

But the fact that you are working on your own healing matters for how you lead. It matters for how you show up in a room with a person who is falling apart. It matters for whether you create genuine safety or just the appearance of it.

Some of the greatest leaders in Scripture were wounded people. Moses with his insecurity. David with his family dysfunction. Paul with his past as a persecutor. The wounds were not the problem. Unexamined wounds were the problem. Wounds they bled on others were the problem.

The Wounded Healer

Henri Nouwen wrote about the concept of the wounded healer—the idea that our own wounds, when honestly faced and tended, become sources of healing for others.[3] This is not the same as bleeding on people. It is the opposite.

The wounded healer has looked in the Mirror. They have seen their wounds clearly. They have sought healing. And from that place of honest engagement with their own pain, they can sit with others in their pain without flinching, without fixing, without fleeing.

When you have done your own work, you can hear someone else's story without being overwhelmed by your own. You can recognize trauma responses because you have recognized them in yourself. You can offer hope for healing because you have experienced healing. Your wound becomes a window through which you see others more clearly—not because you have transcended your pain, but because you have walked through it honestly.

This is what happened with Pastor Andrew.

As Andrew healed, his leadership transformed. He became gentler with his staff. He learned to delegate. He stopped micromanaging. He preached about grace with a vulnerability he had never shown before—because now he was actually experiencing it himself, not just teaching a concept he had memorized.

His church's trauma-responsive transformation accelerated—because the senior leader was no longer unconsciously sabotaging it with his own unhealed wounds. The people in his congregation who were carrying their own invisible weight began to sense something different in their pastor. Something safer. Something real. They could not have named it, but their nervous systems recognized it. This person has been where I am. This person understands.

The Mirror came before the Window. And it changed everything.

Then Look Through the Window

Once you have done your own work—or at least begun it in earnest—you can look through the Window with clear eyes.

Now when you see the person who cannot seem to trust, you recognize a nervous system that learned early in life that trust is dangerous. You do not take it personally. You understand.

Now when you see the person who cannot stop performing, you recognize someone whose childhood taught them that love must be earned. You offer unconditional acceptance. You break the pattern.

Now when you see the person who explodes in anger, you recognize an amygdala stuck in threat-detection mode. You do not escalate. You de-escalate. You create safety.

Now when you see the person who is distant and disconnected, you recognize dissociation—a survival mechanism that once kept them safe. You do not push. You wait. You prove yourself trustworthy.

You stop seeing sin and start seeing wounds. You stop judging and start understanding. You stop offering prescriptions that do not work and start asking the question that opens doors: What happened to you?

This is what the Window looks like when the Mirror has been cleaned. Not perfection. Not clinical expertise. Just clarity. The kind of clarity that comes from knowing your own story well enough that you do not accidentally project it onto someone else's.

The Mirrors Work Together

Now let me connect this back to the previous chapter. The Faith Community Trauma-Responsive Index—the organizational assessment—is the church looking into its collective mirror. It is the congregation asking: Who are we really? What is our actual capacity to help wounded people? Where are our blind spots?

The personal Mirror and the organizational Mirror reinforce each other. A church full of leaders who have done their own work will produce a healthier, more honest organizational assessment. And an honest organizational assessment will often surface the need for personal work that leaders have been avoiding.

This is why transformation fails when churches try to skip the Mirror phase. They jump straight to programs and trainings without ever honestly examining themselves—personally or organizationally. They look through the Window at the wounded world without ever cleaning the glass. And they end up projecting their own unhealed stuff onto the people they are trying to help.

The Promise

Here is what I can promise you.

If you do this work—if you look honestly in the Mirror, if you seek healing for your own wounds, if you become a wounded healer rather than a wounded wounder—everything changes.

You will see people more clearly. You will respond with greater wisdom. You will create genuine safety because you have found safety yourself. You will model the very transformation you are inviting others into. You will lead from health rather than from hidden pain.

And whatever comes next in your church's journey—the training, the assessments, the structural changes we will discuss in the chapters ahead—will have a foundation. It will not be a program bolted onto an unhealthy system. It will be an expression of people who have done their own work and are now equipped to help others do theirs.

The Mirror comes before the Window. Always.

Secure your own oxygen mask. Then help others.

Endnotes

1. The Adverse Childhood Experiences (ACE) questionnaire, developed by Felitti and Anda in the original CDC-Kaiser ACE Study (1998), remains the most widely used tool for assessing childhood trauma exposure.

2. EMDR (Eye Movement Desensitization and Reprocessing) was developed by Francine Shapiro in 1987 and has become one of the most extensively researched treatments for trauma.

3. Henri J. M. Nouwen, *The Wounded Healer: Ministry in Contemporary Society* (Garden City, NY: Doubleday, 1972).

Chapter Fifteen

Becoming a Certified Trauma-Responsive Church

> "For which of you, intending to build a tower, does not sit down first and count the cost, whether he has enough to finish it?"
>
> –Luke 14:28

You have read this far. You have seen the crisis. You understand the framework. You have looked in the Mirror—personally and organizationally. And now you are asking the practical question:

How do we actually do this?

This chapter provides the roadmap. I am going to walk you through the transformation journey—not with enough detail for you to do it alone, but with enough clarity for you to understand what you are committing to and whether your church is ready to make that commitment.

But before I describe the framework, let me tell you why I believe it will work—and why you should believe it too.

Why a Corporate Transformation Expert Is Writing This Chapter

I spent 15 years leading large-scale organizational transformations at Fortune 100 companies—Coca-Cola, Johnson & Johnson, and others. I co-authored a book called Corporate Transformation based on a six-year study of how successful organizations fundamentally reinvent themselves. I did not study transformation from the outside. I led it from the inside—with thousands of employees, entrenched cultures, skeptical leadership, competing priorities, and limited budgets. Every obstacle your church will face on this journey, I have faced in boardrooms and factory floors and global headquarters.

Here is what I learned across all of those engagements: transformation follows patterns. The organizations that succeed share certain characteristics. The ones that fail share different characteristics. And the differences are predictable.

Successful transformation requires committed senior leadership—not delegation. It requires prepared hearts before training begins. It requires the right sequence at the right pace. It requires equipping people with real skills, not just awareness. And it requires visible measurement so progress does not stall in the messy middle.

The organizations that fail? They skip steps. They rush timelines. They delegate the hard work to middle management. They launch training before anyone understands why. They treat transformation as a program instead of a cultural shift.

These patterns hold whether you are transforming a pharmaceutical company or a church. The context changes. The human dynamics do not.

The framework I am about to describe—what we call the Trauma-Responsive Faith Community Transformation Framework—is built on those 15 years of real-world transformation experience, adapted specifically for faith communities.[1] It is informed by decades of trauma research, consultation with clinical experts, and the practical realities of church life.

I want to be transparent: we are early. As of this writing, two churches are piloting the full framework. This book is, in some ways, ahead of the data. I do not have 20 case studies to show you. I cannot point to a church that completed the journey three years ago and show you their before-and-after numbers.

What I can tell you is this: the methodology underneath this framework is not new. It is not theoretical. It has been tested and refined across some of the largest, most complex organizations in the world. I have seen it work when nothing else did. And I have adapted it with the same rigor for the church—because the church deserves the same quality of thinking that Fortune 100 companies get.

What Already Exists and Where It Falls Short

In Chapter 12, I pointed you toward resources that any church can access right now—books, the SAMHSA framework, the ACE questionnaire, immediate steps pastors can take. Those resources are valuable. They are where you start.

But here is the ceiling I have observed: Awareness without a transformation framework produces well-informed inaction. Churches read the books. Pastors take the training. Everyone nods and agrees that trauma is real and the church should respond. And then nothing structurally changes. The sermons go back to normal. The small groups run the same way. The counseling referrals do not materialize. The awareness fades.

This is not because the resources are bad. It is because awareness is Level 2 on a four-level journey. And most existing programs stop at Level 2. They give you knowledge. They do not give you a systematic path from knowledge to organizational transformation.

SAMHSA's framework—Realize, Recognize, Respond, Resist Re-traumatization—is excellent as a conceptual model. But it was designed for clinical and social service settings, not faith communities. It does not address the unique theological, structural, and cultural dynamics of churches. It does not tell a pastor how to preach differently, restructure small groups, or navigate a congregation in which half the elders think trauma is a secular distraction from the gospel.

Individual training programs—and there are good ones—equip individuals. But individual knowledge does not produce organizational change. I have watched this pattern repeat across every industry I have worked in: you can train every manager in the building, and if you have not addressed the systems, the culture, and the leadership commitment, the training evaporates within 90 days.

What UACT's framework adds is the piece that is missing everywhere else: a systematic, phased, measured path from where your church is now to where it needs to be. Not just awareness. Transformation.

The Six Pillars of Faithful Transformation

Effective transformation requires six elements working together. These are not optional add-ons—they are structural requirements. Weakness in any one undermines all the others. I have seen every one of these validated across 15 years of corporate transformation work, and they apply to churches with equal force.

Pillar 1: Pastoral Leadership Commitment. This cannot be delegated to a ministry director or counseling staff. The congregation watches where leadership invests attention—and follows. If the senior pastor treats this as important, the church will follow. If it is delegated away, it becomes "just another program." The senior pastor and elder board must personally complete trauma awareness training before the initiative launches. The Mirror comes before the Window.

Pillar 2: Clear Vision Connected to Mission. A compelling vision that connects trauma-responsive transformation to the church's core mission—not as an addition to what you do, but as a fuller expression of who you already are. This is not a mental health initiative. This is Luke 4:18-19 made practical: "The Spirit of the Lord is on me. . . to bind up the brokenhearted, to proclaim freedom for the captives." Becoming trauma-responsive is becoming more like Jesus, not adding a program.

Pillar 3: Prepared Hearts. Systematic preparation of the congregation before training begins. This is where most transformation efforts fail—they launch training before the congregation understands why. Stigma must be addressed. Questions must be answered. Hearts must be warmed to receive what is coming. The message: 70% prevalence means this is not about "those people"—it is about us.

Pillar 4: Right Sequence, Right Pace. Phased implementation that builds foundations before scaling. Attempting to skip steps or compress timelines dramatically increases failure risk. I have watched billion-dollar companies destroy promising initiatives by rushing the timeline. Churches are no different. Rushing creates resistance. Patience builds momentum.

Pillar 5: Equipped Shepherds. Practical training that gives leaders the knowledge and skills they need to respond effectively—not just awareness, but capability. UACT certification equips pastors, elders, counselors, small group leaders, and youth workers with trauma-responsive skills. This is not about becoming therapists—it is about knowing when to walk alongside and when to refer, what to say and what never to say, how to create safety, and how to avoid re-traumatization.

Pillar 6: Visible Progress. Regular measurement of progress with visible reporting. What gets measured gets attention. What gets attention gets done. The Faith Community Trauma-Responsive Index provides baseline assessment and progress tracking. Regular updates to leadership and congregation build accountability and celebrate wins.

Understanding the six pillars tells you how to transform your church. Understanding the three levels that follow tells you who does the healing once the transformation is underway.

The Three Levels of Trauma Care

One of the most common fears I hear from pastors when they engage with this framework is this: *Are you asking me to become a therapist?*

The answer is no. Emphatically, no.

What we are asking is something far more achievable—and far more powerful. We are asking you to become a triage nurse.

Think about how a hospital emergency room works. When you walk through the doors, a triage nurse meets you first. That nurse is not a surgeon. They are not a psychiatrist. They are not going to perform your procedure. But they are trained to do the single most important thing in the entire system—they can see the wound, assess its severity, provide immediate stabilized care, and know with precision when to call in the next level of expertise. Without the triage nurse, the surgeon is overwhelmed and the person with the treatable injury waits six hours next to someone in cardiac arrest.

The church, for 2,000 years, has had no triage nurses. Pastors have been handed the full spectrum of human suffering—from mild anxiety to severe complex PTSD—with no training to distinguish between them, no framework to assess severity, and no clear referral pathway when the wound exceeds their capacity. The result is predictable: either they try to treat everything with spiritual aspirin, or they refer everything out and abandon the wounded to a secular system that has no idea what to do with the spiritual dimension of their pain.

The UACT model builds a three-level system that solves this. Each level has a defined role, a defined scope, and a defined handoff. Nobody is being asked to exceed their training. Nobody is being abandoned without a next step.

Level One
The Practitioner

This is the new class of healer UACT Academy is creating. Pastors. Church counselors. Chaplains. Lay leaders. Foster parents. Educators. These are not licensed clinicians. They are trained, UACT-certified first responders who can see the wound, provide trauma-responsive first aid—a listening ear, a safe relationship, basic psychoeducation about trauma and its effects—and know when what they are seeing requires a higher level of care.

The Level One responder does not diagnose. They do not treat complex clinical disorders. They do not attempt EMDR or somatic therapy or any specialized clinical intervention. What they do is extraordinarily valuable and currently almost entirely absent from the church: they see the person, they do not shame them, they provide a stable and safe relational presence, and they know when to say *I think you need someone with more specialized training than I have, and I am going to help you find that person.*

That single skill—recognizing the wound and knowing when to refer—would transform the church's capacity to serve its wounded members overnight.

Level Two
The Licensed Clinician

Licensed clinical therapists with specialized training in evidence-based trauma modalities—EMDR, Accelerated Resolution Therapy, somatic experiencing, trauma-focused cognitive behavioral therapy. These clinicians will have a minimum of a master's degree. These are the practitioners who treat what Level One identifies as beyond their scope: complex PTSD, dissociative disorders, severe trauma presentations, and cases requiring deep clinical expertise. UACT's CTRT credential—Certified Trauma Responsive Traumatologist—ensures that the therapists in this Level are not only clinically trained but also trauma-responsive in the fullest sense. They are searchable by zip code in the UACT provider database, and the UACT benevolence fund reimburses only CTRT-certified clinicians, ensuring quality control throughout the system.

Level Three
Board-Certified Trauma Responsive Coach

Someone building a business offering healing services to individuals and organizations. No degree required.

The power of this system is not in any single level. It is in the handoffs.

Right now, a wounded person in your congregation has two options: talk to a pastor who has no clinical training, or navigate a complex and expensive mental health system entirely on their own. The three-level model builds a bridge between those two extremes. The pastor sees the wound. He knows where to send the person. The person arrives at the next level of care already stabilized, already understood, already accompanied—not abandoned into a system that feels foreign and frightening.

We are not asking your church counselor to be a therapist. We are not asking your pastor to diagnose PTSD. We are asking them to be the triage nurse—the trained, present, compassionate first point of contact who ensures that no one who walks through your doors bleeds out in the waiting room.

That is a role the church was always meant to play. We are simply giving it a name, a training curriculum, and a certification that proves it has been done right.

The Phased Journey

The transformation unfolds in three phases over approximately 12 months. This timeline assumes a congregation of around 3,000 members. Smaller churches may complete the journey faster; larger or multi-site churches should plan for 18 months. The sequence remains constant; the timeline flexes with size.

Before the phases begin, there is an engagement and assessment period—completing the baseline FCTI assessment[2], understanding the scope of trauma in your specific community, defining which ministries and leaders are involved, and establishing a partnership agreement with milestones and accountability.

Phase 1: Foundation (Months 1-3)

Phase 1 establishes the conditions for successful transformation. The most critical element—and the first action—is preparing the congregation's hearts.

This phase begins with a comprehensive communication strategy. This will be one of the most significant initiatives your church has ever undertaken. It touches every member. It addresses sensitive personal histories. Without careful preparation, resistance will undermine everything that follows. The communication must normalize the conversation, de-stigmatize seeking help, connect to mission, and build anticipation rather than anxiety.

During this phase, all pastoral staff and elders complete certification—before any broader rollout begins. This accomplishes three things: personal awareness as leaders examine their own histories, content credibility so leaders can speak authentically about what they have learned, and visible commitment so the congregation sees that leadership went first.

A transformation team is assembled—a cross-ministry group including the senior pastor, pastoral care director, small groups leader, youth and children's ministry leader, worship leader, and congregant representatives. And quick wins are implemented—visible early changes that demonstrate commitment and build momentum.

By the end of Phase 1, 100% of pastoral staff and elders should be certified, the communication campaign should be launched with broad awareness, the transformation team should be operational, at least three quick wins should be implemented and visible, and the FCTI score should have improved by at least ten points from baseline.

Phase 2: Equipping (Months 4-8)

Phase 2 extends trauma-responsive capability throughout the ministry leadership and begins systematic changes to how the church operates.

All ministry leaders and key volunteers complete certification—small group leaders, youth and children's ministry workers, pastoral care team members, hospitality leaders, recovery ministry leaders. For a church of 3,000, this typically means certifying 25 to 35 key leaders—the shepherds who have direct contact with the congregation.

Based on training insights, systematic improvements are made to ministry practices: small group guidelines for creating safety, worship practices that consider trauma survivors, counseling protocols for intake and referral, youth ministry approaches that recognize children experiencing trauma in real time. These changes are not mandated by UACT—they are implemented by leadership based on their awareness and training.

A congregational awareness module is deployed church-wide—available through weekend services, small groups, or on-demand viewing. It explains why the church is pursuing this transformation, introduces basic concepts, shares stories of hope, and explains how to access help.

By the end of Phase 2, 80% of ministry leaders should be certified, ministry practices should be redesigned for priority areas, the congregational awareness module should be completed by at least 60% of active members, counseling referral utilization should have increased, and the FCTI score should reach 76 or higher—crossing the threshold from Trauma-Aware to Trauma-Informed.

Phase 3: Integration (Months 9-12)

Phase 3 moves the church from Trauma-Informed to Trauma-Responsive through active healing programs and prevention initiatives.

Healing ministry is developed or enhanced: a therapy benevolence fund helping members access professional trauma treatment, support groups for grief and recovery and trauma survivors facilitated by trained leaders, a peer support network of trained wounded healers walking alongside others, contemplative practices like somatic regulation and lament services.

Prevention programs are established to break the intergenerational cycle: parenting support to equip parents to raise resilient children, marriage enrichment addressing trauma dynamics in relationships, trauma-responsive training for foster and adoptive parents caring for wounded children, age-appropriate education for youth.

The sanctuary extends beyond church walls: free trauma-responsive care offered to the community, partnerships with local schools and social services and mental health providers, the church becoming known as a healing resource rather than just a worship venue.

By the end of Phase 3, active healing programs should have measurable participation, prevention infrastructure should be operational, at least one community partnership should be established, documented stories of healing and transformation should exist, and the FCTI score should reach 114 or higher—crossing the threshold to Trauma-Responsive. The church becomes eligible for UACT Trauma-Responsive Faith Community Certification.

Not Every Church Has to Do Everything at Once

I want to address something directly, because I know what some of you are thinking: This sounds like a massive undertaking. My church cannot commit to this right now.

I hear you. And I want you to know: the full Level 4 certification is the destination, but it is not the only way to begin.

Here is what I have learned from 15 years of corporate transformation: the biggest enemy of progress is not resistance.[3] It is the belief that if you cannot do everything, you should do nothing. That all-or-nothing thinking kills more initiatives than active opposition ever will.

So let me describe what is possible for churches at different stages of readiness.

If your church can commit to the full framework: Follow the phased journey I just described. Partner with UACT for guidance, assessment, and certification. Aim for Level 4 over twelve to eighteen months. This is the gold standard.

If your church is not ready for full commitment but wants to move: Start with Phase 1 only. Get leadership certified. Launch the communication campaign. Take the FCTI baseline assessment. See where you are. You can pause after Phase 1 and still be dramatically ahead of where you started. When the time is right, resume with Phase 2.

If you are a smaller church with limited staff and budget: Consider forming a regional cohort—three to five churches in your area pursuing the journey together. Share training costs. Learn from each other. Hold each other accountable. Smaller churches often have an advantage in transformation because there are fewer layers of bureaucracy and the senior pastor has direct relationships with most of the congregation.

If you are a solo pastor or a church plant: Focus on the personal Mirror work from the last chapter. Get trained yourself. Begin integrating trauma-responsive awareness into your preaching and counseling. Build the foundation now so that when your church grows, trauma-responsive practice is in the DNA from the start.

The point is to move. Not perfectly. Not completely. But to move. Every step up the four-level framework matters. A church at Level 2 is serving its wounded members better than a church at Level 1. A church at Level 3 is changing lives that a church at Level 2 is still missing. Progress, not perfection.

After Certification: Staying the Course

Certification is not the finish line. It is a milestone. The real question is whether transformation becomes permanent or fades once the initiative energy dissipates.

I have watched this exact pattern in corporate settings: a company invests heavily in transformation, hits its targets, celebrates the win—and three years later, the culture has drifted back to where it started. The reason is always the same: they treated transformation as a project with an end date instead of a permanent shift in how the organization operates.

Here is how churches sustain what they have built.

Annual reassessment. Every certified church completes the FCTI annually. This is not optional. It is how you catch drift before it becomes decline. Your score will fluctuate—staff turnover, leadership changes, and competing priorities are realities. The assessment keeps you honest.

Continuous certification. New ministry leaders and key volunteers complete certification as they come on board. Trauma-responsive capability is not a one-time training—it is a requirement for anyone who shepherds others in your church.

Ongoing congregational awareness. New members need the same foundation your existing members received. Integrate trauma awareness into your new member process. Keep the conversation alive from the pulpit—not as a weekly drumbeat, but as a consistent thread in your teaching.

Peer networks. Certified churches connect with each other to share what they are learning—what is working, what is not, what they wish they had known. UACT facilitates these networks because isolated churches lose momentum. Connected churches sustain it.

Accountability. UACT maintains an active relationship with certified churches. If a reassessment shows significant decline, we work with leadership to understand why and develop a recovery plan. Certification is not a plaque on the wall. It is an ongoing commitment.

Addressing Common Concerns

When churches consider this journey, certain questions and reactions arise consistently. Let me address them directly.

"Is this just another program that will fade away?" It will be if leadership treats it that way. That is why pastoral commitment is the first pillar. I have watched corporate initiatives worth millions of dollars die because the CEO delegated them to a VP and moved on. If your senior pastor is not personally invested, do not start. Wait until they are.

"This seems too psychological. What about Scripture and prayer?" We are not replacing Scripture and prayer—we are adding understanding that helps them work more effectively. God heals in many ways: through prayer, through Scripture, through community, and through the healing knowledge He has given us through science. Faith and neuroscience are not enemies—they are partners.

"We have too many competing priorities right now." Every organization I have ever worked with said this. Every single one. There will never be a season with no competing priorities. The question is not whether this competes with other things—it does. The question is whether 70% of your congregation carrying invisible wounds is important enough to prioritize. If not now, when?

"We do not have the staff capacity." This framework is designed to work within existing staff structures. You are not hiring a trauma department. You are equipping the people you already have—pastors, small group leaders, youth workers—with new skills. The transformation team is drawn from existing leadership. The time investment is real, but it is not a new hire.

"We cannot afford it." Training costs money. I will not pretend otherwise. But consider what you are already spending on the consequences of unaddressed trauma: staff turnover from burnout, counseling crises that consume pastoral time, members leaving because they did not find help, programs that serve symptoms but never touch root causes. The cost of doing nothing is not zero—you are just paying it in ways you have not measured. For smaller churches, regional cohorts can share costs significantly.

"What about confidentiality?" All personal participation is completely voluntary and confidential. Leadership should never know who uses counseling referrals or attends support groups. The only thing that is visible is that your church is becoming a safer place for everyone.

"I do not have trauma. Why should I care?" Even if you do not have personal trauma, people you love probably do—your spouse, your children, your friends, the person sitting next to you in the pew. And as a ministry leader, you are almost certainly ministering to trauma survivors without knowing it. This equips you to help them more effectively.

"Is focusing on trauma just making excuses for sin?" Absolutely not. Understanding trauma does not excuse behavior—it explains it. When we understand what happened to someone, we can help them heal rather than just telling them to try harder. Jesus never shamed the wounded. He touched them, saw them, and healed them.

The First 30 Days

If you are ready to begin, here is what the first thirty days look like.

In the first week, the senior pastor and executive pastor complete the FCTI baseline assessment together, understand the scope of trauma in your congregation, identify a champion for the initiative, and begin planning how to introduce this to the congregation.

In weeks two and three, the communication strategy is developed, transformation team members are identified and invited, pastoral staff certification is scheduled, and the counseling referral network research begins.

In week four, the communication strategy is approved by leadership, the transformation team holds its first meeting, and the first quick win is identified and implementation planned.

The full framework includes detailed guidance for every phase, milestone deliverables, and the complete journey through certification. That level of detail is available at UACTNOW.com.

Is Your Church Ready?

Not every church is ready to begin this journey. Readiness requires certain conditions.

The senior pastor must be personally committed—not delegating to staff, but championing this as a priority. The elder board or governing body must be supportive—not just tolerating but actively endorsing the initiative. Leadership must be willing to go first—completing their own certification before asking anyone else to participate. The church must be willing to invest real resources—staff time, training costs, and potentially counseling benevolence funds. And there must be patience for a 12-to-18-month journey—understanding that culture change cannot be rushed.

If these conditions exist, your church is ready. If they do not, the most loving thing I can tell you is to wait until they do. Starting before you are ready leads to failure, and failure makes future attempts harder.

The Invitation

What I have described in this chapter is the architecture of transformation. It is built on methodology proven across some of the most complex organizations in the world, adapted for the specific terrain of the local church. But architecture without action is just a beautiful drawing.

If your church is ready to move from architecture to construction—to actually begin this journey—here is the next step.

Go to UACTNOW.com and complete the Faith Community Trauma-Responsive Index. It takes less than an hour. When you submit it, UACT will personally review your results and email you a report written specifically for your church—your score on the four-level spectrum, your gaps, and a suggested pathway forward. That report is not generated by a machine and sent automatically. A real person who understands this work will look at your answers and give you something worth having.

The report also includes an offer to schedule a Pathway Conversation with our team—a focused call to walk through your results and answer the question your leadership needs answered: what would it actually take for your church to move to the next level? No sales pitch. No pressure. Just clarity about where you are and what the path forward looks like.

I want to be honest about something else: you cannot successfully do this alone. Not because you lack intelligence or commitment, but because you lack objectivity about yourself and expertise in trauma-responsive transformation. That is not a criticism. It is simply the nature of organizational change. The churches that complete this journey are the ones that get help doing it.

Start at UACTNOW.com. The rest follows from there.

What Is at Stake

Every day, approximately 1,401 Americans die from health conditions attributable to childhood trauma. Some of them are in churches right now, bleeding in pews where no one can see the wound.

The churches that move first will become what they were always meant to be: sanctuaries where the wounded actually heal, not just places where they are told to try harder. They will become known not for what they are against, but for what they heal. They will attract the broken, the addicted, the desperate—because those are the people Jesus attracted, and they recognize His presence when they see it.

The churches that wait will keep doing what they have always done: offering spiritual solutions to neurobiological wounds, watching people try harder and fail harder, losing the very people Jesus came to save.

This is the church's Kairos moment.[4]

The question is not whether becoming trauma-responsive aligns with Jesus's mission. "The Spirit of the Lord is on me . . . to bind up the brokenhearted, to proclaim freedom for the captives." That was His mission statement. This is what He came to do.

The question is whether your church will do it.

This concludes Part Four: From Diagnosis to Prescription. We have moved from understanding the crisis to seeing the framework, from looking in the Mirror to mapping the journey from Level 1 to Level 4.

But I do not want to end this book with a framework. Frameworks are necessary—without them, good intentions produce nothing. But frameworks are not the point. People are the point. Lives are the point. The wounded sitting in your pews right now, hoping against hope that someone will finally see them—they are the point.

Part Five is called The Promise. In it, I want to offer a view of what becomes possible if a church makes this journey. I want to tell you about the lives that could change, the families that might heal, the communities that transform when a church finally becomes what it was always meant to be.

Because the bleeding in the pews is not the end of the story. It is the beginning. And the ending—the promise—is more beautiful than you can imagine.

Endnotes

1. The Trauma-Responsive Faith Community Transformation Framework was developed by United Against Childhood Trauma (UACT) in 2025–2026. Full documentation available at www.uactnow.com.

2. FCTI scoring thresholds: 0–37 (Trauma-Unaware); 38–75 (Trauma-Aware); 76–113 (Trauma-Informed); 114–150 (Trauma-Responsive).

3. Michael Menard, David Nielson, C. Richard Panico, and Noel Sobelman, *Corporate Transformation: A Guide to Success and Survival* (Independently Published, 2021).

4. Paul Tillich, *The Protestant Era* (Chicago: University of Chicago Press, 1948). The Greek concept of *kairos* as distinguished from *chronos* receives seminal theological treatment in this work.

PART FIVE
THE PROMISE

CHAPTER SIXTEEN

The Return on Mission

> "Now to him who is able to do immeasurably more than all we ask or imagine . . ."
>
> –Ephesians 3:20

JUST IMAGINE.

It is Sunday morning at Grace Community Church, a congregation of 3,000 members in a mid-sized American city. The parking lot fills. Families stream through the doors. The worship band warms up. On the surface, it looks like any other church on any other Sunday.

But something is different here. Something has changed.

Two years ago, the senior pastor read a book about childhood trauma. He learned that 70% of adults were carrying wounds from their earliest years—wounds that showed up as anxiety, depression, addiction, failed relationships, chronic illness, and early death. He did the math: in his congregation of 3,000, that meant roughly 2,100 people were possibly carrying invisible wounds into the sanctuary every Sunday.

Twenty-one hundred people. Bleeding in the pews.

He could not unsee it. So he did something about it.

Grace Community became a trauma-responsive church. The transformation took 18 months. It required investment, training, and sustained commitment. It was not easy.

But now, two years later, the return on that investment is visible everywhere.

Measuring What Matters

In my other book—Bleeding in the Boardroom—I wrote about the financial return on investment of trauma-responsive transformation in corporations. Two trillion dollars in annual costs. Measurable improvements in productivity, retention, healthcare spending, and profitability. The business case is overwhelming.

But churches do not measure success in dollars. They measure success in mission.

So let me reframe the question. When a church invests in becoming trauma-responsive—the training, the time, the counseling benevolence funds, the organizational change—what does it get back? What is the return on mission?

The return is measured in six outcomes. Each of them is real. Each of them is observable. And each of them connects directly to why your church exists in the first place.

People stay. The exodus that has been hemorrhaging American churches reverses. Wounded people who were leaving because the church could not help them start staying because it can. The back door closes—not because you are trapping people, but because they are finding what they came for.

People heal. Not just spiritually—though that happens too—but neurobiologically. The depression lifts. The anxiety quiets. The addictions loosen their grip. The relationships repair. The bodies recover. Real healing. Measurable healing. The kind you can see in someone's face when they finally understand what happened to them and realize that healing is possible.

People grow. Spiritual formation that was blocked by unresolved trauma finally becomes possible. People who could not experience God's love because their nervous systems could not receive it begin to feel what they only knew intellectually. Faith deepens because the barriers have been removed. Remember what we learned in Chapter 3—a nervous system stuck in survival mode cannot access the prefrontal cortex functions needed for reflection, trust, and spiritual growth. When healing quiets the amygdala, the whole person opens up.

People serve. Healed people become healers. The woman who found freedom from her attachment wounds becomes the small group leader who helps others find their own freedom. The man who broke free from addiction mentors others on the same journey. The couple whose marriage was saved teaches the next marriage enrichment class. Healing multiplies.

Families transform. When parents heal, children inherit health instead of wounds. The intergenerational transmission of trauma—the cycle that has passed pain from generation to generation for as long as anyone can remember—is interrupted. A family line that was headed toward continued suffering is redirected toward thriving.

Communities change. A trauma-responsive church does not keep its healing within its walls. It extends into the community—free counseling resources, parenting classes, support groups open to anyone. The church becomes known not for what it believes but for how it heals. And people come.

These six outcomes are not aspirational language for a brochure. They are the observable markers of a church that has completed the journey we described in the last chapter. And every one of them has a face.

Thomas

Thomas is 47 years old. He has been a deacon at Grace Community for 12 years. Everyone knows him as reliable, steady, always willing to help. What no one knew—what Thomas himself barely acknowledged—was that he had been fighting a secret battle with alcohol for most of his adult life.

It started in college. A few drinks to take the edge off. By his thirties, it was a nightly ritual—three or four glasses of whiskey after the kids went to bed. By his forties, he was hiding bottles. His wife suspected. His doctor warned him. But Thomas kept it together. He showed up. He performed. He served.

He never connected his drinking to his childhood. His father had been an angry man—not physically abusive, but emotionally volatile. You never knew which version of Dad was coming home. Thomas learned early to walk on eggshells, to manage other people's emotions, to disappear when things got tense. He thought he had moved past all that. He was wrong.

When Grace Community began its transformation, Thomas sat through the congregational awareness session expecting to hear about other people's problems. Instead, he heard his own story. The facilitator explained how children who grow up in unpredictable environments develop hypervigilant nervous systems—the amygdala stuck on high alert, always scanning for danger, creating a need for something, anything, to quiet the noise. Alcohol. Food. Work. Religion. Something to bring the nervous system down from its permanent state of emergency.

For the first time in his life, Thomas understood. He was not weak. He was wounded. The whiskey was not a moral failure—it was self-medication for a dysregulated nervous system that had been stuck in survival mode since he was eight years old.

Thomas entered the church's recovery support group—not the old model that focused only on willpower and accountability, but a trauma-responsive group that addressed the root cause, not just the symptom. The church's benevolence fund helped him access a trauma-responsive therapist. Three months of therapy including Accelerated Resolution Therapy (ART) intervention processed the childhood experiences he had buried for 40 years.

Today, Thomas has been sober for 14 months. Not white-knuckling it. Not counting days with dread. Actually sober—because the wound that drove his drinking has finally begun to heal. His marriage has transformed. His relationship with his adult children has deepened. His service as a deacon now flows from health rather than from the compulsive need to earn his worth.

Thomas would have died early. The statistics are clear: men with his ACE score and his drinking pattern lose an average of 15 to 20 years of life. Heart disease. Liver failure. Accidents. Suicide. One of those outcomes was waiting for him.

Now it is not.

That is the return on mission. One life. Outcome number two: people heal.

The Real Costs and Why Churches Hesitate

Before I go further, let me be honest about what this costs. Because I respect you enough not to pretend it is free.

Money. Training is not free. Certification for leadership and key volunteers costs real dollars. A counseling benevolence fund means ongoing budget commitment. For a mid-sized church, expect to invest meaningfully in the first year—less in subsequent years as the infrastructure is established, but never zero.

Time. Leadership certification takes time away from other priorities. The communication campaign takes planning. The transformation team meetings take hours. The congregational awareness modules take scheduling. Every hour spent on this is an hour not spent on something else.

Emotional energy. This work surfaces pain. It will surface pain in your leaders who do their Mirror work. It will surface pain in your congregation as awareness grows. There will be tears in your building that were not there before—not because you caused the pain, but because you finally created a space safe enough for people to show it.

Institutional risk. Some members will not understand why you are doing this. A few will push back. You may lose people who think this is "too psychological" or "not biblical enough." That is real, and it hurts.

Competing priorities. Your church already has a full calendar. Youth ministry needs attention. The building fund is behind schedule. The missions trip is in three months. Adding trauma-responsive transformation to the list means something else gets less attention—at least for a season.

I am not minimizing any of this. Every one of these costs is real.

But here is what I have learned across 15 years of leading organizational transformation: the cost of change is always visible. The cost of staying the same is always hidden. You can see the training budget on a spreadsheet. You cannot see the marriages that quietly disintegrated because no one understood the wound underneath the fighting. You can count the hours spent in transformation team meetings. You cannot count the people who slipped out the back door because your church could not help them. You can feel the awkwardness of surfacing pain in your congregation. You cannot feel the silent suffering of 2,100 people who have been carrying their wounds alone.

The cost of doing nothing is not zero. You are paying it right now. You just cannot see the invoice.

Jennifer

Jennifer is 34. She joined Grace Community three years ago after years of church-hopping—never staying anywhere long, never feeling like she belonged. She would get involved, then pull back. Get close to people, then disappear. She had a pattern she did not understand and could not break.

Jennifer's mother left when she was six. Just gone one day. No explanation. No goodbye. Her father did his best, but he was overwhelmed and emotionally unavailable. Jennifer learned that people leave. That attachment is dangerous. That the safest thing is to never need anyone too much.

Her attachment wound showed up everywhere: in friendships that never deepened, in romantic relationships she sabotaged before they could hurt her, in churches she left before anyone could really know her. She was lonely in a crowd. Isolated in community. Hungry for connection but terrified of it.

At Grace Community, something different happened. Her small group leader had been through the church's trauma-responsive training. When Jennifer started to pull back—missing meetings, dodging invitations—the leader did not take it personally or let her disappear. Instead, she reached out with a patient, persistent, non-demanding presence.

"I notice you've been quieter lately," she said. "I'm not going anywhere. Whenever you're ready."

That sentence—"I'm not going anywhere"—broke something open in Jennifer. For the first time, someone saw her pattern and did not abandon her for it. Someone stayed.

Jennifer is still at Grace Community. She has been in the same small group for two years—the longest she has stayed anywhere since childhood. She is in therapy, working on her attachment wounds. She has started to let people in.

The old Jennifer was on a trajectory toward a lifetime of isolation, depression, and the cardiovascular disease and autoimmune conditions that research links to chronic loneliness. The new Jennifer is building the connections that will literally extend her life.

That is the return on mission. One small group leader who knew enough to stay. Outcome number one: people stay.

What Success Actually Looks Like

Let me step back from the individual stories and describe what measurable success looks like across a congregation.

Grace Community has 3,000 members. Approximately 2,100 of them carry childhood trauma. Before the transformation, almost none of them were receiving trauma-responsive care. The church was doing its best, but its best was spiritual solutions for neurobiological wounds.

After the transformation, the church has systems in place to actually help. Trained leaders who can recognize trauma responses. Support groups that address root causes. Referral networks to professional therapists. Financial assistance for treatment. A culture where seeking help is celebrated rather than stigmatized.

Not everyone will access these resources. Not everyone is ready. But over the first two years, approximately 15% of the congregation—450 people—have engaged with some form of trauma-responsive support. Some joined support groups. Some accessed therapy through the referral network. Some simply had a conversation with a trained small group leader that changed how they understood themselves.

Four hundred and fifty people whose trajectory has shifted.

Research tells us that effective trauma treatment reduces healthcare costs, decreases substance abuse, lowers depression and anxiety, improves relationships, and extends life expectancy. If even 10% of those 450 people experience significant healing—45 people—the impact is staggering.

Forty-five people who will not die early from trauma-related illness. Forty-five families that will not be shattered by addiction or suicide or divorce. Forty-five sets of children who will inherit health instead of wounds.

And those 45 healed people? They become healers themselves—outcome number four. They share what they have learned. They walk alongside others in their own healing journeys. The ripple extends outward—from individual to family to congregation to community.

This is not return on investment measured in dollars. This is return measured in mission fulfilled. In lives reclaimed. In generations redirected.

The Martinez Family

Carlos and Maria Martinez have been married for nineteen years. They have three children. From the outside, they looked like a model Christian family. From the inside, they were drowning.

Carlos grew up in a home where conflict meant violence. When his parents fought, things got broken. Sometimes people got broken. He learned that anger is dangerous—that the safest response to conflict is withdrawal. Shut down. Disappear emotionally until the storm passes.

Maria grew up in a home where she was invisible. Her parents were physically present but emotionally absent. She learned that if you want connection, you have to pursue it relentlessly. Chase it. Demand it. Because if you do not, no one will come.

Put these two people in a marriage, and you get a devastating dance. Maria pursues. Carlos withdraws. Maria pursues harder, feeling abandoned. Carlos withdraws further, feeling attacked. Neither understands why they cannot connect. Neither sees that they are not fighting each other—they are fighting childhood wounds neither knew they had.

When Grace Community offered its marriage enrichment program—redesigned with trauma awareness—Carlos and Maria enrolled as a last resort. They were 18 months from divorce. Their children were already showing signs of anxiety and behavioral issues, absorbing their parents' dysregulation the way children always do.

In the program, they learned about attachment styles. They saw, for the first time, that their conflict pattern was not about the specific issues they fought over—money, parenting, household responsibilities—but about deeper wounds they had each brought into the marriage. Carlos was not cold and uncaring; he was terrified of conflict because conflict once meant danger. Maria was not needy and demanding; she was desperate for the connection she never received as a child.

Understanding changed everything. Carlos learned to stay present in conflict instead of disappearing. Maria learned to give space instead of pursuing. They each entered individual therapy to address their childhood wounds. Their marriage is still hard work—nineteen years of patterns do not change overnight—but they are finally working on the right problem.

Their children are watching. They are learning what healthy conflict looks like. What repair looks like. What staying and working through difficulty looks like. The intergenerational cycle of trauma that was about to claim another generation is being interrupted.

That is the return on mission. One marriage saved. Three children whose futures have been rewritten. Outcome number five: families transform.

Pastor Andrew

You met Pastor Andrew in an earlier chapter—the senior pastor whose workaholism and perfectionism were unexamined trauma responses, who wept when he finally saw himself clearly, who entered therapy and watched his leadership transform.

What happened to Andrew's church when its leader healed?

Staff turnover dropped by half. For years, Andrew's micromanagement and impossible standards had driven talented people away. When he learned to delegate, to trust, to lead from health rather than fear, people started staying. The institutional knowledge that had been walking out the door began to accumulate.

Congregational engagement increased. Andrew's preaching changed—still excellent, but now vulnerable. He began sharing his own struggles, his own journey, his own humanity. People who had admired him from a distance began to trust him up close. The congregation that had respected a perfect leader began to love a real one.

And the transformation accelerated. Because Andrew had done his own Mirror work, he could lead the church through its transformation without unconsciously sabotaging it. His buy-in was authentic. His teaching was personal. His example was visible.

Andrew took a creative and bold step. He wore a T-shirt with a large number 7 on the front and back when he introduced the congregation to the trauma-responsive kickoff service. Andrew's ACE score is 7. No hiding. No pretending. Just a leader who went first.

The church followed because the shepherd went first.

That is the return on mission. A leader who became more effective by becoming more human. Outcome number three: people grow—including the people at the top.

Now Multiply

Grace Community is one church. There are approximately 380,000 churches in America.

What if just 1% of them—3,800 churches—became trauma-responsive? If the average church has 200 members, that is 760,000 people in congregations with trauma-responsive systems. If 15% engage with support, that is 114,000 people receiving help. If 10% experience significant healing, that is 11,400 lives transformed.

What if 10% of churches—38,000—became trauma-responsive? The numbers scale: 7.6 million people in trauma-responsive congregations. Over a million engaging with support, and 114,000 lives transformed.

Remember that childhood trauma kills approximately 1,401 Americans every day. That is 511,000 per year. If the church—just the church, not the healthcare system, not the government, just the community of faith—could reduce that number by even 5%, we would save more than 25,000 lives per year.

That's 25,000 people who would have died but did not. Because churches learned to see. Because they chose to heal instead of just to preach. Because they became what they were always meant to be.

That is the return on mission at scale. And it is not fantasy. It is math. It is possibility. It is the promise.

The True Measure

The return on mission of a trauma-responsive church is Thomas, finally free from the addiction that was killing him slowly. It is Jennifer, learning to let people in after a lifetime of self-protective isolation. It is Carlos and Maria, saving their marriage and changing the trajectory of their children's lives. It is Pastor Andrew, leading from health instead of hidden pain.

The return is the moment when someone who has been stuck for decades finally understands what happened to them—and realizes, for the first time, that healing is possible.

The return is the teenager who does not become another overdose statistic because a youth pastor recognized the signs and knew what to do.

The return is the grandmother who breaks down in tears because her grandson just got married—and she never thought she would live to see it, because her own wounds had convinced her she would die young like everyone else in her family.

You cannot put a dollar value on these moments. But you can count them. You can see them. You can hold them up and say: This is what becomes possible when the church learns to heal.

Just imagine. Your church, transformed. Your congregation, healing. Your community, changing. Lives extended. Families restored. Generations redirected from suffering toward thriving.

This is not fantasy. This is what becomes possible when a church sees the bleeding in its pews and does something about it.

This is the return on mission. And the question is not whether it is worth it, it's whether your church is ready to claim it.

But this vision—beautiful as it is—remains incomplete. One church helping its own members is good. But what if churches did more than heal themselves? What if they became the leading edge of a movement to heal humanity?

That is the vision of the next chapter.

Endnotes

1. Julianne Holt-Lunstad et al., "Loneliness and Social Isolation as Risk Factors for Mortality: A Meta-Analytic Review," *Perspectives on Psychological Science* 10, no. 2 (2015): 227–237.

2. The pursuer-distancer dynamic in couples is extensively documented in attachment research, particularly in the work of Susan M. Johnson and her development of Emotionally Focused Therapy (EFT). See Susan M. Johnson, *The Practice of Emotionally Focused Couple Therapy: Creating Connection* (New York: Brunner-Routledge, 2004); see also Johnson, *Hold Me Tight*, previously cited.

3. Mark Chaves et al., *National Congregations Study Cumulative Dataset*, Association of Religion Data Archives, 2021, https://www.thearda.com/data-archive?fid=NCSIV.

Chapter Seventeen

The Fourth Ripple

> "You are the light of the world. A city set on a hill cannot be hidden."
>
> –Matthew 5:14

Drop a stone into still water and watch what happens.

The stone creates a splash at the point of impact. But the effect does not stop there. Ripples extend outward in concentric circles, each one larger than the last, until they reach the farthest edges of the pond.

A single stone. An entire surface transformed.

Healing works the same way. When one person heals from childhood trauma, the effect ripples outward—to their family, their workplace, their community. When a church becomes trauma-responsive, the ripples extend further still. And when churches across a nation begin healing their communities, the ripples become a wave.

In the last chapter, I showed you the return on mission when a church heals its own members. In this chapter, I want to show you the fourth ripple—what becomes possible when churches stop thinking of healing as something they do for their congregation and start thinking of it as something they bring to the world.

The Four Ripples

Transformation moves outward in four concentric circles.

The First Ripple: The Individual. This is where it starts. One person—Thomas, Jennifer, Maria, Andrew—encounters trauma-responsive care and begins to heal. The wound that has shaped their life for decades finally receives treatment. The patterns that seemed permanent begin to shift. Every person who heals becomes a carrier of healing to others. They understand what it means to be wounded and what it means to recover. The healed become healers—not because they have achieved perfection, but because they have walked the path and can guide others on it.

The Second Ripple: Leadership. When leaders heal, organizations transform. A pastor who has done their own trauma work leads differently—with more patience, more empathy, and more capacity to create safety. An elder board whose members understand their own wounds governs with greater wisdom. The second ripple multiplies the first. One healed leader influences dozens. Those leaders influence hundreds. What happens at the top shapes everything below.

The Third Ripple: The Congregation. When a critical mass of individuals and leaders have experienced healing, the culture of the entire congregation shifts. Stigma around mental health dissolves. Vulnerability becomes normalized. Seeking help becomes a sign of strength rather than weakness. The congregation becomes a genuine sanctuary—not just a place where people gather, but a place where wounded people actually find healing. The third ripple reaches everyone, even those who never access formal support. They benefit from trained small group leaders, trauma-sensitive worship, preaching that acknowledges real suffering, and a culture that does not shame struggle.

The Fourth Ripple: The Community. This is where the vision expands beyond the church walls. A trauma-responsive church does not hoard its healing. It extends outward—to the neighborhood, the city, the region. The church becomes part of the community's healing infrastructure, working alongside therapists, schools, hospitals, and social services to address the trauma crisis that no single institution can solve alone.

The fourth ripple is where the church fulfills its calling to be salt and light in the world. Not by positioning itself above other institutions, but by bringing something to the table that no other institution can match.

What the Church Uniquely Offers

Let me be clear about something. The church is not the only institution that can help trauma survivors. Professional therapists do essential clinical work that churches cannot and should not attempt to replace. Schools, hospitals, social services, and government programs all play critical roles. The mental health system—broken as it is—serves millions of people the church will never reach.

The church is not here to lead the trauma response. It is here to join it—and to bring something to the partnership that no one else has.

What does the church uniquely offer?

Scale. There are approximately 380,000 churches in America, embedded in virtually every community—urban, suburban, rural. They already have buildings, volunteers, organizational structures, and weekly gatherings. They already have relationships with millions of Americans. No government program could build this infrastructure from scratch. No nonprofit could replicate it. The church is already there—on every Main Street, in every neighborhood, woven into the fabric of American life.

Community. Healing does not happen in 50-minute clinical sessions alone. It happens in relationship—in the daily experience of being known, being safe, being connected. The church offers something no clinic can provide: ongoing community. Weekly presence. People who show up again next Sunday. Small groups that meet for years. Relationships that persist through difficulty. For trauma survivors whose core wound is disconnection, this is not a bonus. It is the medicine.

Accessibility. The mental health system in America cannot scale to meet the need. There are not enough therapists. The ones who exist are often unaffordable. Wait times stretch into months. People in crisis fall through the cracks. The church can serve as a complement to professional treatment—a first line of support, a community of care that walks alongside people during the long journey of healing, a bridge to clinical resources for those who need them.

Motivation. Most institutions serve people because it is their job. The church serves people because it is its calling. That distinction matters—not because paid professionals care less, but because mission-driven communities sustain effort differently. When budgets get cut and grant cycles end, churches are still there. When the program is over, the community remains.

The church is not replacing anyone. It is filling a gap that no one else can fill—the gap between clinical treatment and daily life, between professional care and ongoing community, between what the system can provide and what wounded people actually need.

You Are Now Entering Your Mission Field

There is a church in Naples, Florida—First Baptist—that has a sign at the exit of their parking lot. As you drive away from the church campus, you pass these words:

YOU ARE NOW ENTERING
YOUR MISSION FIELD

That sign captures something essential. The mission is not inside the building. The mission is outside—in the neighborhoods, the work-places, the schools, the hospitals, the streets. The building is where you gather and equip. The world is where you serve.

For too long, churches have thought of trauma ministry as something they do inside their walls—for their members, within their programs, contained in their congregations. That is good. That matters. But it is not enough.

The mission field is full of wounded people who will never join your church. They are not looking for religion. They are looking for help.

They are the single mother working two jobs whose childhood abuse shows up as chronic anxiety she cannot explain. They are the teenager whose trauma is manifesting as addiction and his parents have no idea why. They are the veteran whose combat trauma sits on top of childhood trauma no one ever asked about. They are the elderly widow whose lifelong depression traces back to things that happened 70 years ago that she has never spoken aloud.

These people are bleeding in your community. They are dying at the rate of 1,401 per day nationwide. And most of them will never walk through your doors on Sunday morning.

What if the church went to them?

What Community Ministry Looks Like

Let me paint a picture of what this could look like in practice.

Free community support groups. The church offers trauma recovery groups, grief support, addiction recovery, and parenting classes—open to anyone in the community, regardless of religious affiliation. No requirement to attend services. No pressure to join. Just help, offered freely.

School partnerships. The church partners with local schools to provide trauma-responsive training for teachers and counselors. Church members volunteer as mentors for at-risk students. The church hosts after-school programs designed with trauma awareness. Children who would never set foot in a church building receive help from people who were equipped by one.

Healthcare connections. The church builds relationships with local hospitals, clinics, and mental health providers. When someone is discharged after a mental health crisis, the hospital knows there is a church that offers ongoing community support—not judgment, not preaching, but the long-term relational care that the clinical system cannot sustain. The church becomes part of the community's healing infrastructure.

Criminal justice ministry. The church offers trauma-responsive support for people exiting incarceration—a population where childhood trauma prevalence exceeds 90%. Reentry programs that address the root cause of criminal behavior, not just its consequences. Mentoring relationships that provide the stable connection many of these individuals never had.

Foster and adoption support. The church becomes a hub for foster families—offering trauma-responsive training, respite care, support groups, and practical help. Every child in foster care has experienced trauma by definition. Churches that equip families to care for these children are doing frontline healing work that changes the trajectory of the most vulnerable lives in our society.

Workplace awareness. Church members who have been trained in trauma responsiveness bring that knowledge into their workplaces. They become informal sources of support and referral in offices, factories, and hospitals across the community. The church's healing ministry extends through its members into every corner of the local economy.

None of this requires anyone to become a believer before receiving help. All of it extends the church's healing ministry beyond its walls into the community that needs it most.

Healing Without Strings

Let me be direct about something that makes some church leaders uncomfortable.

When I talk about churches extending healing to their communities, I am not talking about bait-and-switch evangelism. I am not talking about offering help as a way to get people into the building so you can convert them. I am not talking about healing as a marketing strategy for church growth.

I am talking about healing because healing is what Jesus did. Full stop.

Look at the Gospels. Jesus healed people constantly, relentlessly. He healed the blind, the lame, the lepers, the demon-possessed. And here is the thing that should reshape how we think about outreach: He did not require belief before He healed. He did not demand conversion as a condition for compassion. He healed people because they were suffering and He had the power to help.

Sometimes healing led to faith. Sometimes it did not. The ten lepers were all healed; only one came back to give thanks. Jesus healed the other nine anyway.

This is the model for trauma-responsive community ministry. Heal because people are suffering. Help because you can. Offer because you have received. Do not attach strings. Do not require attendance. Do not make church membership the price of admission to your support groups.

Here is what I want to say carefully, because it matters.

When a person has been carrying a wound since childhood—when their nervous system has been stuck in survival mode for 30 or 40 or 50 years—that wound does not just affect their health and their relationships. It affects their capacity to believe. I have talked to countless people who said some version of this: There cannot be a God. If there were, He would not have let this happen to me. That is not a theological failure. It is a trauma response. When the world was cruel to them at age five, when the people who were supposed to protect them became the ones who hurt them, when no one came to help—their nervous system drew a conclusion: I am alone. No one is coming. There is no one looking out for me. That conclusion gets generalized. It extends from the people who failed them to the God who, in their experience, also failed them. The wall goes up. And no amount of preaching, no argument, no apologetics can get through that wall—because the wall is not intellectual. It is neurobiological. It lives in the amygdala, not the prefrontal cortex.

But when healing happens—when the wound finally receives the care it needed all along—something shifts. The nervous system begins to quiet. The wall begins to come down. And questions that were sealed shut for decades reopen. Not because anyone forced them open. Not because healing was a trick to get someone to believe. But because a person who is no longer drowning can finally lift their head and look around.

Some of those people will explore faith. Some will not. That is their journey, not ours to engineer. But we should not pretend that healing and spiritual openness are unrelated. They are deeply connected—because the same wound that broke a person's body and mind often broke their capacity to trust that anything good exists beyond what they can see.

The church does not heal people so they will believe. The church heals people because they are suffering. But when suffering lifts, doors open that no one could have predicted. And if the church has been the community that walked with them through the darkness, it will be the natural place they turn to when they are ready to explore the light.

That is not evangelism through manipulation. It is evangelism through faithfulness. And there is all the difference in the world between the two.

The Banner on the Building

I have a vision. I imagine driving through an American city and seeing banners on church buildings. Not banners advertising sermon series or holiday services.

Banners that say:

TRAUMA-RESPONSIVE CHURCH
Everyone Is Welcome

Imagine what that would mean to someone driving by. Someone who has never felt welcome in a church. Someone who assumes that religious people will judge them for their struggles. Someone who is desperate for help but has no idea where to find it.

They see that banner and they know: This is a place that understands. This is a place that helps. This is a place where I might actually find what I need.

The banner is not just a sign. It is a statement. It says: We see you. We know what you are carrying. We have tools to help. And we will not make you jump through hoops to receive care.

I imagine a future where that banner becomes a recognized symbol—like a hospital's red cross or a pharmacy's green sign. A marker that tells people: Help is here. A designation that communities learn to trust.

This is what UACT certification makes possible. When a church achieves Trauma-Responsive status, it earns the right to fly that banner. It has demonstrated—through rigorous assessment, not self-declaration—that it has the training, the systems, and the culture to actually help wounded people heal.

The banner becomes a promise. And the community learns that the promise is real.

The Movement

Imagine the ripple extending further still.

One church becomes trauma-responsive and begins healing its community. That church shares what it has learned with other churches in the area. A regional network emerges. Churches that once competed for members now collaborate for healing.

The network becomes a movement. The movement spreads across denominations. Baptist and Methodist and Catholic and Pentecostal churches—divided by doctrine—unite around the mission of healing. They share training resources. They refer people to each other. They speak with a common voice about the trauma crisis. The divisions that have fragmented the church for centuries become less important than the mission that unites them.

The movement attracts attention. Media coverage shifts from church scandals to church healing. The narrative changes. The church—so often portrayed as judgmental, hypocritical, out of touch—becomes known for something different. Something beautiful. Something that makes people say: "Whatever I think about religion, those people are doing real good."

The movement influences policy. When churches across a city demonstrate that community-based trauma support works, local government takes notice. Partnerships form. Resources follow. The church becomes a recognized partner in public health—not because it claimed the spotlight, but because it showed up and delivered results.

The Return to Identity

Here is the deepest truth of this chapter.

When churches extend healing beyond their walls, they are not adding something new to their mission. They are returning to something ancient.

The early church was known for healing. Not just spiritual healing—though that too—but physical, emotional, practical healing. When plagues struck Roman cities, Christians stayed to care for the sick while others fled. When infants were abandoned, Christians rescued them. When the poor were hungry, Christians fed them. The church grew not because it had better arguments but because it demonstrated better love.

Somewhere along the way, we lost this. The church became more known for what it opposed than what it healed. More known for judgment than compassion. More known for words than works.

Becoming trauma-responsive is not innovation. It is recovery. It is the church remembering who it was always supposed to be: a sanctuary for the wounded, a hospital for the sick, a community where the broken find healing and the healed become healers.

The fourth ripple is not new. It is the oldest ripple of all. And it is time for it to expand again.

We have come a long way in this book. From the invisible wound to the church's blindness. From the hemorrhage to the transformation. From the promise of individual healing to the vision of churches bringing healing to the world.

One chapter remains. It is time to talk about the moment we are in—and the choice before you.

Endnotes

1. Rodney Stark, *The Rise of Christianity: A Sociologist Reconsiders History* (Princeton: Princeton University Press, 1996).

2. Nena Messina and Christine Grella, "Childhood Trauma and Women's Health Outcomes in a California Prison Population," *American Journal of Public Health* 96, no. 10 (2006): 1842–1848, https://pubmed.ncbi.nlm.nih.gov/17008581/.

3. Mark Chaves et al., *National Congregations Study Cumulative Dataset*, Association of Religion Data Archives, 2021, h ttps://www.thearda.com/data-archive?fid=NCSIV. Combined weekly attendance exceeding 100 million Americans.

Chapter Eighteen

The Kairos Moment

> "Behold, now is the favorable time; behold, now is the day of salvation."
>
> –2 Corinthians 6:2

What You Now Know

You have traveled through this book. You have seen things you cannot unsee. Let me walk you back through what we discovered together, because the weight of it matters.

We said the thing the church has too often left unsaid: that the wounding of a child is evil, that Scripture treats it as one of the highest offenses against God, and that silence in the presence of that evil is no longer the silence of blindness—it is the silence of choice. The church's neutrality on childhood trauma is over. The only question that remains is whether your church will be among the first to break the silence or among the last.

We began with Shannon sitting in the first row of her church, smiling on the outside and hemorrhaging on the inside—and we learned that her story is not the exception. It is the norm. 70% of the adults in any congregation carry at least one adverse childhood experience. In a church of 500, that is 350 people. In a church of 3,000, that is 2,100. Bleeding in the pews. Invisible to almost everyone.

We looked at the data and saw the hemorrhage for what it is. People are leaving the church at staggering rates—and while the reasons are complex, one of the deepest is this: wounded people came looking for healing and did not find it. The back door is wide open, and the church has been watching people walk through it without understanding why.

We went inside the brain and learned what trauma actually does. The amygdala stuck on high alert. The prefrontal cortex overridden. The hippocampus unable to file the past where it belongs. The nervous system locked in survival mode for years, for decades, for a lifetime. We learned that trauma is not a character flaw or a spiritual failure—it is a neurobiological injury. And we saw what happens when that injury goes untreated: the total disintegration of a person's physical health, mental health, social connections, and spiritual life.

We examined the theology that created blind spots—2,000 years of well-intentioned doctrine that inadvertently told wounded people to pray harder, believe more, and try again. We saw how the ancient pattern—the gods are angry, so you must have sinned—still echoes in churches that mistake trauma responses for moral failures.

We counted the cost. A loss of $12 trillion annually. A loss of 1,401 lives per day. The leading cause of death in America, hiding in plain sight beneath the diseases it generates. We saw that the church has been treating symptoms while the root cause bleeds on.

We learned that the shepherds are bleeding too—that the 70% prevalence does not skip the pulpit. That pastors carry their own invisible wounds into their ministry, and those wounds shape everything they do and everyone they lead.

We watched the exodus unfold—Daniel, Sarah, Michelle—and understood that people are not leaving the church because they have lost faith. They are leaving because the church could not help them with the thing that was destroying them.

We sat with addiction and saw it clearly for the first time—not as moral weakness but as self-medication for a nervous system that never found peace. We grieved with families like the Caldwells, watching trauma pass from grandmother to granddaughter like an inheritance no one asked for.

Then we turned a corner. We discovered that resources already exist for any church ready to start—and we learned why starting is necessary but not sufficient. We looked in the Mirror, personally and organizationally, and understood that leaders cannot create safety they have never experienced. We mapped the journey from Trauma-Unaware to Trauma-Responsive—a journey built on methodology tested across 15 years of Fortune 100 transformations. We saw the return on mission: lives extended, families healed, generations redirected. And we cast a vision of the fourth ripple—churches bringing healing beyond their walls into communities that are desperate for it.

You know all of this now. You cannot unknow it.

The question is: What will you do with what you know?

Two Futures

There are two possible futures from this moment.

In one future, you close this book and return to normal. The information settles into the category of "interesting things I've read." Sunday comes. You preach. The wounded sit in your pews, unseen. Some leave. Some stay and suffer. Some die early, and you officiate their funerals never knowing that their deaths were preventable. Years pass. Nothing changes. The bleeding continues.

In the other future, you act. You look in the Mirror—personally and organizationally. You begin the journey toward becoming trauma-responsive. It takes time. It requires investment. It is harder than doing nothing. But slowly, things shift. Your leaders are trained. Your culture changes. People who were suffering in silence find help. Lives are extended. Families are healed. The intergenerational cycle of trauma begins to break. Your church becomes what it was called to be.

Two futures. One choice. Yours to make.

Why I Wrote This Book

Adam and Patrick. They both had ACE scores of 6—the kind of childhood trauma that shortens life expectancy by 20 years. They were not weak. They were wounded. The drugs were not moral failure. They were self-medication for pain that never received proper treatment.

For years, I judged them. I could not understand why they kept making destructive choices. Why they could not just stop. Why they seemed determined to ruin their lives.

Then I learned what I have shared with you in this book. And I understood.

Too late for them. But not too late for others.

If I had known then what I know now, my brothers might still be alive. If someone in their world—a pastor, a youth leader, a small group facilitator—had understood childhood trauma and known how to help, the trajectory might have been different. The wound might have been treated before it became fatal.

I wrote this book for the Adams and Patricks in your congregation. The ones who are bleeding right now. The ones who still have time.

I wrote it because I do not want you to stand at another funeral, years from now, and realize that you could have helped but did not know how.

Now you know how.

The Excuses

I know the objections. I have heard them all.

"We don't have the resources."

You have enough to start. The journey begins with leadership commitment, not budget lines. The resources follow the priority.

"Our people aren't ready."

Your people are already wounded. They are ready to be seen. They are waiting to be helped. The question is whether leadership is ready to lead.

"This isn't our core mission."

Binding up the brokenhearted is exactly your core mission. It was Jesus's mission statement. It must be yours.

"We'll get to it eventually."

Eventually is too late for some of the people in your pews right now. While you wait, they suffer. While you delay, some of them die. Kairos does not wait for eventually.

The excuses are understandable. Change is hard. The status quo is comfortable. But the excuses do not change the math. They do not stop the bleeding. They do not bring back the ones we lose while we hesitate.

The Invitation

Join us. Join the movement of churches that are choosing to see. That are doing the hard work of becoming what they were always meant to be.

Here is what I am asking you to do. Not eventually. Now.

Go to UACTNOW.com and complete the Faith Community Trauma-Responsive Index. It takes less than an hour. When you submit it, UACT will personally review your assessment and email you a results report written specifically for your church, your level on the spectrum, your specific gaps, and a suggested path forward. Not an automated printout. A real person will look at what you submitted and give you something you can actually use.

The report includes an offer to schedule a Pathway Conversation with our team—30 minutes to walk through your results together and answer the question that matters most: what does the next step actually look like for your church?

If you are a senior pastor, take the assessment with your executive pastor or your elder board. Have the conversation. Look at the results together.

If you are not the senior pastor—if you are a small group leader, a deacon, a youth worker, a concerned member—complete the assessment yourself and bring it to your pastor. Say: I read this book. I took this assessment. I think we need to talk. Sometimes the door opens from the inside.

The first step is the assessment. Take it this week.

For Those Still Bleeding

One more word—not for pastors and church leaders, but for anyone reading this book who recognizes themselves in these pages. Anyone who has been bleeding in the pews. Anyone who has wondered if something is fundamentally wrong with them because church has not healed what church is supposed to heal.

It is not your fault.

The wound you carry is real. The pain you feel is valid. The fact that spiritual solutions alone have not healed you does not mean you lack faith. It means you have a neurobiological injury that requires neurobiological treatment—and there is no shame in that.

Find help. Seek a trauma-responsive therapist. Join a support group. Tell someone safe what you are carrying. Healing is possible. It may be slower than you want. It may be harder than you hoped. But it is possible.

And if your church does not understand—if they tell you to pray harder or believe better or try more—know that they are blind, not cruel. Forgive them for their blindness. And find help anyway.

You are worth healing. Your life is worth extending.

Your future is worth fighting for.

Kairos is approaching. You can see him now. Swift, winged, that single lock of hair falling over his forehead. He is close. In a moment, he will be within reach.

This is the church's decisive hour. The moment when we could finally see what we have been missing. When we could finally help those we have failed to help. When we could finally become what we were always meant to be.

The forelock is before you.

Grasp it.

The bleeding has gone on long enough.

Appendix A

Read this section carefully, because it is easy to misread. Nothing here says prayer does not work. It says prayer was never designed to do this particular job by itself. A believer with a broken femur prays and then goes to the surgeon, and no one calls that a failure of faith. The same is true of a nervous system shaped by childhood trauma. Prayer sustains. It is often the only thing that has been keeping the person upright. But the bone still has to be set.

Summary
Everything the Church Leader Needs to Know

This summary is for readers who want the essential argument of this book in a few pages. It is not a substitute for the full text—the stories, the science, and the details matter—but if you need the core message quickly, or if you want to share this book's thesis with someone who may not read the whole thing, this is where to start.

The Crisis You Didn't Know You Had

Childhood trauma is the leading cause of death in America. Not heart disease. Not cancer. Childhood trauma—through its downstream effects of addiction, suicide, chronic disease, and high-risk behavior—kills approximately 1,401 Americans every day. That is more than 511,000 people per year; more Americans annually than COVID killed in its deadliest year.

Seventy percent of American adults experienced at least one adverse childhood experience (ACE) before age eighteen. In your congregation, that means seven out of every ten people in the pews are carrying invisible wounds that affect their health, their relationships, their families, and their capacity to experience the abundant life Jesus promised.

This is not a counseling issue affecting a small group of particularly troubled members. It is a crisis hiding in plain sight—sitting in your pews every Sunday, bleeding invisibly while the church prescribes remedies that do not work.

What It Is Costing Your Church

The American church is hemorrhaging people. The back door is wide open, and the wounded are walking through it. In a congregation of 2,000:

- 1,401 members carry childhood trauma (70%)
- 420 members have ACE scores of 4+, putting them at dramatically elevated risk for depression, addiction, and chronic disease
- 144 members have ACE scores of 6+, facing life expectancy reductions of 20 years
- Unknown numbers have already left—or are planning to—because they found no healing

These are not statistics. They are people. People who show up on Sunday smiling, singing, serving—and bleeding. People whose depression gets labeled as weak faith. Whose anxiety gets treated as insufficient trust in God. Whose addiction gets condemned as moral failure. Whose inability to forgive gets preached at rather than understood.

The economic toll is staggering. McKinsey puts the cost of poor workforce health globally at up to $12 trillion a year, and the research on childhood adversity specifically puts its own economic burden in the trillions when you account for healthcare spending, lost productivity, addiction treatment, criminal justice costs, and reduced quality of life.

The church is not cruel. The church is blind. Blind to wounds that are neurobiological, not spiritual. Blind to injuries that prayer alone cannot heal—not because prayer does not work, but because prayer is not designed to rewire a dysregulated nervous system. That is like expecting prayer to set a broken bone without ever touching the fracture.

Why "Pray Harder" Isn't Enough

Childhood trauma physically changes the brain. The amygdala becomes hyperactive—a smoke detector that goes off when someone makes toast. The hippocampus is affected, making it much harder to file traumatic memories as "past" rather than "present." The prefrontal cortex—responsible for emotional regulation and impulse control—develops differently. The nervous system locks into fight, flight, or freeze and stays there for years, for decades, for a lifetime.

This is why the standard prescriptions fail:

- "Just trust God" asks someone whose brain cannot reliably distinguish past danger from present safety to override their survival system with a decision.

- "Have more faith" asks someone whose amygdala is flooding their system with cortisol to feel safe enough to surrender control.
- "Just forgive" asks someone whose prefrontal cortex is impaired to perform complex emotional processing.
- "Read your Bible more" asks someone in chronic fight-or-flight to concentrate when their nervous system is scanning for threats.

These prescriptions are not wrong—they are incomplete. They are spiritual solutions to neurobiological injuries. And when they do not work, the wounded person concludes that they are the problem. That their faith is deficient. That God has abandoned them. And eventually, they leave.

This is the ancient pattern that echoes through history: the gods are angry, you must have sinned, try harder. Two thousand years of well-intentioned theology that inadvertently tells wounded people their suffering is their fault. It is not. The question the church must learn to ask is not "What is wrong with you?" but "What happened to you?" Ask it as an invitation, never a demand, and know your state's reporting duties and your referral list before you do.

The Solution: Becoming Trauma-Responsive

Churches exist on a four-level maturity spectrum:

Level 1: Trauma-Unaware. The church does not recognize trauma's presence or impact. No awareness. Punitive or dismissive responses to trauma symptoms. The vast majority of American churches are here—not because they do not care, but because they have never been shown what to look for.

Level 2: Trauma-Aware. The church recognizes that trauma exists and affects its members, but has not yet changed its practices or systems in response. This is where most churches land after reading a book or attending a conference. Awareness is necessary but insufficient.

Level 3: Trauma-Informed. The church has trained its leadership, begun modifying its practices, and started building systems to identify and respond to trauma. Ministry leaders understand what trauma does and how to avoid re-traumatizing people. The church is actively changing how it operates.

Level 4: Trauma-Responsive. The church has fully integrated trauma-responsive practices into every dimension of its ministry—preaching, counseling, small groups, youth ministry, worship, and community outreach. It has trained leadership at every level. It has systems for assessment, referral, and ongoing support. It has extended its healing ministry beyond its walls into the community. The church has become a genuine sanctuary—a place where the wounded actually heal.

The critical distinction: Trauma-aware asks "Do we know trauma exists?" Trauma-informed asks "Have we changed how we operate?" Trauma-responsive asks "Are we actively healing people?" Most churches claiming to address trauma are aware at best. The gap between knowing and doing is where the bleeding continues.

UACT (United Against Childhood Trauma) has developed the Faith Community Trauma-Responsive Index (FCTI)—a 150-point assessment tool that measures a church's capacity across six domains and maps it to these four levels. The assessment provides an honest baseline and a measurable path forward.

The Transformation Pathway

Becoming trauma-responsive is not a workshop. It is a transformation—one that requires leadership commitment, structural change, and sustained investment. The pathway follows a methodology built on 15 years of leading organizational transformations at Fortune 100 companies including Coca-Cola and Johnson & Johnson, adapted specifically for faith communities.

The transformation unfolds in three phases:

Phase 1: Foundation (Months 1-3). Pastoral staff and elders complete certification first—because leaders cannot create safety they have never experienced themselves. They looked in the Mirror before the Window, meaning they looked inward before they looked outward. A comprehensive communication strategy prepares the congregation. Quick wins build momentum.

Phase 2: Equipping (Months 4-8). All ministry leaders and key volunteers complete certification—small group leaders, youth workers, and pastoral care teams. Ministry practices are systematically redesigned with trauma awareness. A congregational awareness module deploys church-wide.

Phase 3: Integration (Months 9-12). Active healing programs launch—therapy benevolence funds, trauma recovery support groups, peer support networks. Prevention programs address the intergenerational cycle. The church extends healing into the community through school partnerships, foster care support, and collaboration with local mental health providers.

The sequence matters. Leaders go first. Hearts are prepared before training begins. Training leads to practice change, not just knowledge. And the timeline varies based on church size—but you cannot skip phases. Churches that try to compress transformation typically spend more time cleaning up the damage.

Not every church can pursue full Level 4 certification immediately. That is fine. Start with Phase 1. Get leadership certified. Take the baseline assessment. See where you are. A church that completes Phase 1 alone is dramatically ahead of where it started. When the time is right, continue the journey.

The Return on Mission

Churches do not measure success in dollars. They measure success in mission fulfilled. The return on this investment is measured in six outcomes:

- People stay. The exodus reverses. The back door closes. The wounded stop leaving because the church can finally help them.
- People heal. Not just spiritually—neurobiologically. Depression lifts. Anxiety quiets. Addictions loosen. Relationships repair. Bodies recover.
- People grow. Spiritual formation that was blocked by unresolved trauma finally becomes possible. A nervous system stuck in survival mode cannot access the brain functions needed for

reflection, trust, and spiritual growth. When healing quiets the amygdala, the whole person opens up.

- People serve. Healed people become healers. The cycle reverses—from pain passed down to healing passed forward.

- Families transform. When parents heal, children inherit health instead of wounds. The intergenerational cycle of trauma is interrupted.

- Communities change. The church becomes known not for what it believes but for how it heals. It extends healing beyond its walls, partnering with schools, hospitals, and social services to bring care to people who will never walk through the doors on Sunday morning.

If just 10% of American churches became trauma-responsive, over 100,000 lives could be transformed annually. That is not projection—that is math. And it is the promise.

What We Are Asking You to Do

Start with seeing.

Go to UACTNOW.com and complete the Faith Community Trauma-Responsive Index. It takes less than an hour. When you submit it, UACT will personally review your assessment and email you a results report written specifically for your church. That report will include your baseline score—where your church actually stands on the four-level spectrum—your gap analysis, your suggested pathway forward, and an offer to schedule a Pathway Conversation with our team. That conversation is a focused 30 minutes to walk through your results and answer the question: what would it actually take for your church to move to the next level?

No automated scores. No generic output. A real person at UACT reviews every assessment before a report goes out.

If you are a senior pastor, complete the assessment with your executive pastor or elder board. Have the conversation. Look at the results together.

If you are not the senior pastor—if you are a small group leader, a deacon, a youth worker, or a concerned member—complete the assessment yourself and bring it to your pastor. Say: I read this book. I took this assessment. I think we need to talk. The assessment is free. The first step is yours.

Why This Matters Now

Every Sunday you wait, the bleeding continues. Every month, more wounded people leave. Every year, the intergenerational cycle perpetuates as parents pass their unhealed wounds to their children.

But this is not just about stopping losses. It is about becoming what the church was always meant to be—a sanctuary where the wounded actually heal. A hospital for the sick, not a museum for the saints. A place where Jesus's promise of rest for the weary is finally, truly delivered.

The churches that move first will become beacons in their communities. They will attract the wounded who have given up on organized religion. They will retain the faithful who were ready to leave. They will transform families and break generational cycles of suffering.

This is the church's Kairos moment—the decisive hour when everything could change. The science is clear. The need is undeniable. The framework exists. The methodology is proven.

The only question is whether you will act.

The bleeding has gone on long enough. It is time to heal.

For the complete methodology, framework, and stories of transformation, see the full text of Bleeding in the Pews.

For immediate next steps, visit UACTNOW.com

The movement begins now.

Join us at www.UACTNOW.com
Together, we will save American childhood.

UACT
UNITED AGAINST CHILDHOOD TRAUMA

United Against Childhood Trauma. The Shot Heard Around the World.

AWARENESS | HEALING | PREVENTION

www.uactnow.com

Acknowledgments

A book like this one does not get written by a person. It gets assembled from countless hours of research and testimony from real people—and most of that testimony was given long before any of us knew there would be a book. My list is long, as it should be.

First, to my Lord, who has been at my side through every part of this, supplying capability I did not have on my own. I did not come to this work qualified for it. He kept providing what the next page required.

Thank you to Emilie, my wife. Writing this book meant I did less of nearly everything else, and Emilie quietly picked up all of it without once making me feel the cost. She has also been the living proof of what these pages argue. Love heals. I did not learn that from the research. I learned it from her and then went looking for the science that explained it.

I thank my brother Jamie, who brought me to the Lord when I was nineteen and has been dripping Jesus on me ever since—and pouring Him on when I needed it most. Some of Jamie's story is in this book. All of it is in me.

To Allison Buehner, my editor and friend: Thank you for understanding not only my words, but the heart behind them. *Bleeding in the Pews* is a better book because of your wisdom, care, and friendship.

To Dr. Glenn Schiraldi, a trusted friend and colleague, who has given this work the benefit of a lifetime spent studying trauma and helping wounded people recover from it. He has been generous with knowledge that took him decades to learn and develop.

To Dr. Robert Rhoton, for insight that runs deeper than almost anyone whom I have worked with, and for holding together a rare combination—clinical rigor and real faith, with no apology offered for either one.

To my pastor, Darren Tyler, for his influence on me and on this book, and for a Foreword that is both beautiful and unflinchingly honest. He wrote it the way he preaches, which is to say he did not spare himself.

To Shannon Tyler, for her courage. She let me tell her story so that other people might recognize their own in it. That is not a small thing and I have tried to be worthy of it.

To the partners at Alliance Practice—Robert Briggs, Lee Manis, and Thomas Bognanno—for counsel that was consistently wise and consistently kind, which is a harder combination than it sounds.

To Candice Rain, CEO of the Arizona Trauma Institute, my friend and business partner, who saw what this could become and decided to build it alongside me.

To my longtime friend Michael Edwards, who keeps teaching me the same lesson until it takes: I must become less so that my Lord can become more.

To my daughters, Laura, Jenna, Melissa, Anna, and Stella. You created the environment in which I thrive. Everything else I have managed to build rests on that.

And finally, to everyone who has told me—in a hallway, in a lobby, in a parking lot after an event—that they are bleeding in the pews. You trusted a near stranger with something you had not told the people closest to you. This book exists because you spoke up. I hope it finds the ones who have not yet found the words.

About the Author

MICHAEL MENARD'S JOURNEY from trauma survivor to the man who exposed the United States' leading cause of death represents one of the most important discoveries in modern public health.

Born into a family of 14 children in Kankakee, Illinois, Menard learned early that survival required both resilience and innovation. Despite growing up in a 900-square-foot home marked by poverty and dysfunction, he channeled his experiences into extraordinary achievement.

His engineering mind revolutionized industries. Over three decades in corporate leadership, Menard earned 14 patents that transformed global manufacturing, rising to worldwide Vice President of Engineering at Johnson & Johnson. His innovations touched millions of lives daily, proving his ability to solve complex problems at massive scale.

But his greatest discovery came much later. While writing his memoir *The Kite That Couldn't Fly* at age 72, Menard realized that what his family endured wasn't simply a "tough childhood"—it was complex trauma with devastating consequences that rippled through generations. Two brothers lost to addiction, multiple family members stalked by depression—each bearing invisible wounds that never healed.

Menard's engineer mind couldn't ignore the patterns. What began as personal revelation became intensive data analysis, ultimately revealing the shocking truth: severe childhood trauma is killing 1,401 Americans daily, a death toll that surpasses accidents, strokes, and diabetes combined.

The discovery that 89% of teen suicide attempts, 85-100% of addiction cases, and 90% of incarcerated individuals trace back to childhood trauma revealed the scope of this hidden epidemic. At a cost of $14 trillion annually—exceeding our defense budget—America faces its greatest public health crisis in history.

Rather than accept this devastating reality, Menard chose to expose and change it. He founded UACT (United Against Childhood Trauma) with an audacious goal: ending the deadliest force in the United States. His comprehensive plan includes awareness, healing, and prevention strategies designed to save those 1,401 daily lives.

Today, Menard brings the same systematic thinking that revolutionized industries to humanity's greatest challenge. His work has gained support from leading trauma experts, including Dr. Glenn Schiraldi, who calls childhood trauma "the largest threat to the well-being of humanity known today."

Menard lives in Tennessee with his wife, Emilie, whose background in early childhood development complements his mission. Together, they represent the powerful combination of lived experience, data analysis, and unwavering determination required to end America's hidden killer.

www.ingramcontent.com/pod-product-compliance
Lightning Source LLC
LaVergne TN
LVHW010712061126
851857LV00014B/1153